THE ABC BLESSING BOOK

ANOINTING,
BLESSING
& COVERING
YOUR
HOME IN
PRAYER

NATALIE S. WOLFE

THE ABC BLESSING BOOK
ANOINTING, BLESSING & COVERING YOUR HOME IN PRAYER

Copyright © 2016 by Natalie Wolfe. All rights reserved. Except for brief quotations for review purposes, no part of this book may be reproduced in any form without prior written permission from the publisher.

Published by Your Family Blessings, LLC | www.yourfamilyblessings.com
Printed in the U.S.A.

ISBN (Print): 978-0-9976062-0-1
ISBN (Kindle): 978-0-9976062-1-8
Library of Congress Control Number (LCCN): applied for

New International Version
Unless otherwise stated, all Scripture quotations are taken from the HOLY BIBLE, NEW INTERNATIONAL VERSION®. NIV®. Copyright© 1973, 1978, 1984, 2011 by International Bible Society. Used by permission of Zondervan. All rights reserved.

New King James Version
Scripture quotations marked (NKJV) are taken from the New King James Version. Copyright © 1982, Thomas Nelson, Inc. All rights reserved.

New Living Translation
Scripture quotations marked (NLT) are taken from the Holy Bible, New Living Translation, copyright 1996, 2004. Used by permission of Tyndale House Publishers, Inc., Wheaton, Illinois 60189. All rights reserved.

New American Standard Bible
Scripture quotations marked (NASB) taken from the New American Standard Bible®, Copyright © 1960, 1962, 1963, 1968, 1971, 1972, 1973, 1975, 1977, 1995 by The Lockman Foundation Used by permission. (www.Lockman.org)

English Standard Version
Scripture quotations marked (ESV) are from The Holy Bible, English Standard Version®, copyright © 2001 by Crossway Bibles, a publishing ministry of Good News Publishers. Used by permission. All rights reserved.

New English Translation
Scripture quoted by permission. Quotations designated (NET) are from the NET Bible® copyright ©1996-2006 by Biblical Studies Press, L.L.C. (www.Bible.org) All rights reserved.

The Message
Scripture quotations marked (MSG) are taken from The Message. Copyright © 1993, 1994, 1995, 1996, 2000, 2001, 2002. Used by permission of NavPress Publishing Group.

Amplified Bible
Scripture quotations marked (AMP) are taken from the Amplified® Bible,
Copyright © 1954, 1958, 1962, 1964, 1965, 1987 by The Lockman Foundation. Used by permission.

GOD'S WORD
Scripture quotations marked (GW) are taken from the GOD'S WORD translation. GOD'S WORD is a copyrighted work of God's Word to the Nations. Quotations are used by permission. © 1995 by God's Word to the Nations. All rights reserved.

Design & Layout by Palm Tree Productions | www.palmtreeproductions.com

To contact the author: www.ABCBLESSING.com

DEDICATION

To Mom—
my faithful prayer warrior who never gave up on God.
The Lord sang hymns to her as she ascended into heaven.

To Swann, Marybeth, and Jenanne—
my faithful encouragers and inspiration for this book.

CONTENTS

IX   Dear Reader
A Word From Natalie

1   Chapter One
Why Prayer?

9   Chapter Two
Blessing Your Home and Family

23   Chapter Three
Praying Through Your Home With Scripture

31   Chapter Four
Your Property and Surroundings

57   Chapter Five
Common Rooms and Living Spaces

79   Chapter Six
Sleeping and Personal Areas

129   Chapter Seven
Utility Spaces

161   Chapter Eight
Property Maintenance

VI | THE **ABC** BLESSING BOOK

171 APPENDIX
Prayer Walk Through Your Home
Alphabetical Index of Prayers
Over Household Objects

    173   THE WALK

    174   **Cleansing & Forgiveness Prayer**

    177   A

                Activity Calendar, Angels, Arts/Design/Crafts

    182   B

                Bed/Sheets/Pillows, Birds, Blankets, Boats, Books/Reading Material, Buildings/Structures, Bushes/Trees

    193   C

                Candles, Cars, Chairs, Chess Set/Board Games, Children's Beds, Child's Dresser, Children's Blinds/Window Coverings, Child's Closet, Child's Mirror, Child's Desk, City Skyline, Clocks, Clouds, Coat/Hat Racks, Colors, Computers/Mobile Devices/Internet/Digital Media

    218   D

                Doors, Draperies/Window Coverings

    220   E

                Eagles, Exercise Equipment

    223   F

                Family Photos/Family Heritage, Fans, Farms, Fences/Gates, Fireplaces, Fish, Flags, Floors, Flowers, Food, Footstools, Fruit

241 G
Glass/Glasses/Cups, Globe/Maps, Grass

249 H
Horses

250 K
Keys

251 L
Lamp/Lights, Land, Lions, Locks/Protection

257 M
Mirrors, Music/Musical Instruments

263 N
Nature Scenes, Needlepoint/Tapestries

266 P
Paths, Pets, Phones, Pictures of Friends/Neighbors, Plants, Plates/Dishes, Positive Words/Messages

276 R
Rivers/Streams, Roads, Rocks

281 S
Sea/Seashore, Sheep/Lambs, Shoes, Sky, Sofa, Sports Equipment/Memorabilia/Trophies, Stars, Stairs/Steps, Statues, Stereo/CDPlayer/iPod™/ Audio Devices, Sun

299 T
Table, Television/DVD Player, Toys

304   V
         Vessels/Vases

305   W
         Water, Windows, Work Desks

313   MEET THE AUTHOR
         Natalie S. Wolfe

Dear Reader

I am so happy you picked up this book. This book and your prayers will change your life and your family's lives forever! My prayer is that you will understand your role and the truth about blesssing. I have been praying you will be empowered to understand:

- the importance of spiritually cleansing your house or living area through prayer,
- asking for forgiveness and inviting the Lord's blessing.

It sounds easy and it is! I have found when God is involved in something, it is not difficult to understand ... thus the title: *The ABC Blessing Book*! My prayer is that you will understand the importance of covering a person, object, house or land with prayer and with the blood of Jesus. Most importantly, I pray that God is honored by your prayers for your family and home.

I often hear people say they're not sure when God is speaking to them and that God is too busy to answer their prayers. This is not true! The number one hindrance to blocked prayer is unforgiveness. Once forgiveness has occurred, invite God's blessing into your home and family and watch Him move! After reading this book, you can expect to receive insight from the Lord about situations and be blessed in new ways you never dreamed possible.

This book is divided into two parts. The first section is the explanation about blessing in simplistic language and prayers for each area of your home. This is followed by an appendix (beginning on page 177) which provides an alphabetical index of sample blessing prayers over specific household obects.

There is no limit to the items you can pray scripture over or the creative ways you can pray with scripture. After all, you are repeating God's words!

It is preferable to pray with two or three people when "Prayer Walking" your home. So if possible, call a prayer partner and get started! You will both be blessed.

Natalie

Please share your blessing stories on our website:
www.ABCBLESSING.com

CHAPTER ONE

Why Prayer?

From the moment we are born we learn the rules of self-reliance as we strain and struggle to show how independent we can be. How many two-year-olds have you heard say, "Me do it"? Asking someone else to control your life is simply counter-intuitive to an independent spirit. But "me do it" disregards the importance of prayer. Prayer is 180 degrees in the opposite direction, something that goes beyond the natural. That's why praying God's blessing on your home is supernatural. It is going beyond your abilities and connecting with God's. So, just what is prayer?

COMMUNICATING WITH THE HEART OF GOD

To begin, prayer is communicating with the heart of God. In other words, it is conversing with God. Every time we pray, we come into contact with the God of the universe in a profound and life-changing way. It is impossible to experience His presence and not be transformed in some way. Thus, we can pray to the God who gives hope (Note: Rom. 15:13) when we face desperate, hopeless circumstances, emotional needs, or when our children need healing. When we, or our children, have made bad choices or need godly friends, God gives us hope through prayer. During our times of need, when we are struggling with unrealized dreams, an unfulfilled life, or sickness, we know God can and will touch our lives when we ask Him (Note: Heb. 4:14-16).

Prayer is telling God we love and need Him in our lives. When we don't pray, we reveal that we think we can handle life on our own. Jesus told us: *"Apart from me, you can do nothing"* (Jn. 15:5), and that's the real truth. Every good gift in your life comes from God (Note: Jas. 1:17). So, prayer should be specific. It includes asking God to meet specific needs, not just general ones.

When we share what is on our hearts with God, we have confidence that He always cares and that He will meet our needs. He has promised to give us what we need, but He still expects us to ask. We are instructed to pray all the time. This includes praying for every specific need in our lives, our family's lives, and those of our friends as well (Note: 1 Thess. 5:17).

PARTNERSHIP WITH GOD

Prayer is partnership with God. God wants us to join with Him concerning everything in our lives, our future, our family situations, as well as our friends' lives. No matter how large or small a prayer request may be, God wants to hear every single thought, request, or concern. In fact, He will not do some things on earth unless we invite Him to do them. That's why we need to pray and pray specifically. Prayer simply brings us closer to God in every aspect of our lives: our homes, our work, and our world.

When we pray, we are inviting God's kingdom (His control in the world) to operate in our lives and our world. Jesus taught us to pray, *"May Your Kingdom come soon, may Your will be done on earth, as it is in heaven"* (Matt. 6:10 NLT). God's will is perfect for us and for the world, but sometimes His will is not being done on earth as it is in heaven. Actually, God wants to delight us, to fulfill us with joy and peace and love, so He waits for us to pray and ask Him to guide our lives, to be involved in our family's lives, our home, and our world. By His own choice, He often limits His works to those circumstances on earth into which He is specifically invited.

> GOD HAS PROMISED TO GIVE US WHAT WE NEED, BUT HE STILL EXPECTS US TO ASK.

Prayer is the privileged role we have been given to ask God's control for each part of our lives. We can do it anytime, anywhere, under any circumstance (Note: Isa. 55:6). We do so by making specific requests based on God's stated desires found in the Bible.

Ludwig Von Beethoven (1870-1727) was one of the world's premier composers. Yet, in his later years, he would spend countless hours playing a broken harpsichord. For all intents and purposes, the instrument was worthless. Keys were missing. Strings were stretched. It was hopelessly out of tune and abrasive to the ears. Nevertheless, the great pianist would play 'til tears flowed down his cheeks.

If you could have seen him then, you would have thought he was hearing the sublime music he was playing. In fact, he was, for during the last ten years of his life, he was deaf. Beethoven could not hear the sound the instrument was making; he could only hear the sound the instrument should have made.[1]

RESTORE, REBUILD, REPAIR

Do you ever feel that your life or family is like that harpsichord, broken, out of tune, and good for nothing more than firewood? Do you ever struggle with feelings of inadequacy while you publicly act like you have it all together? Is your world out of tune, perhaps even broken beyond repair? What do you suppose would happen if you truly asked God to fix everything in your life? He has promised to restore everything you lost, everything the enemy has taken from you as well as from your family. When God restores, He always improves, increases, and multiplies the blessings many times over. He wants us to gain much more than we have lost (Note: Joel 2:25). Believe me. Beautiful, restored, healing music can resonate from your life and family once again, as you ask His blessing into every part of your home. That is what this book is really about.

> ***Unless the Lord builds the house, its builders labor in vain.***
> PS. 127:1

The Hebrew word translated as builds in this verse can also be translated rebuilds or repairs.[2] The Master of the universe does not discard the broken instrument of our lives. No, He loves to repair them so symphonies of life can once again flow from us and from our families.

I trust you will use this walking guidebook as a kind of manual for inviting God's blessing into your life and home. In Jesus' name:

- Your home will be more loving because God is love (1 Jn. 4:8).

- Your home will have more peace because you invited the Prince of Peace to reign (Isa. 9:6).

- Your home will experience more laughter and joy because the fruit of the Spirit is love, joy, and peace (Gal. 5:22).

- Your home will be a place of patience, a place to experience harmonious relationships because you have actively asked the Lord to rule and reign (Eph. 5:2; Eph. 3:17).

- Your home can be safe from the onslaught of the enemy because the Lord of the universe will crowd out anything not from Himself (Eph. 6:10-12).

- Your home will be magnetic—attracting the good, healthy, wholesome life you desire, and repelling anything destructive, damaging, or bad for your family (Ps. 34:8-10).

I am excited you want to bless your family. I wish we could be sitting across from each other, sharing our stories over tea. We both have the same desire, to see our families blessed beyond what we could think or even imagine. And that comes as we diligently seek God in prayer for our spouses, our children, and all those who come into our homes.

The Bible offers three significant reasons to invite God's blessing upon our families and homes:

1. **He has a plan.** We can understand the heart of God for us.

   "For I know the plans I have for you," declares the Lord, "plans to prosper you and not to harm you, plans to give you hope and a future. Then you will call upon me and come and pray to me,

> *and I will listen to you. You will seek me and find
> me when you seek me with all your heart."*
> JER. 29:11-13

God invites us to bless our families so that we might experience His plans to give us a future and a hope. The Lord invites us to seek because we will find His blessing when we do.

2. **He wants to bless you and your family.** God has promised incredible blessings for our families if we will only ask. Our part is to ask; God's part is to answer.

> *Call to me and I will answer you and tell you great
> and unsearchable things you do not know.*
> JER. 33:3

3. **He wants to answer your prayers.** It is a promise from our Lord Jesus Christ.

> *If you remain in me and my words remain in you,
> ask whatever you wish, and it will be given you.
> This is to my Father's glory, that you bear much
> fruit, showing yourselves to be my disciples.*
> JN. 15:7,8

Do you need a miracle in your family? Ask. Do you need protection? Ask. Do you need God's blessing as you make decisions, face the future, or plan your finances? Ask. Whatever your need, God's Word has the answer. God says He will bless you by answering—and He will never resent you for asking (Note: Jas. 1:3-5). As for God repairing, rebuilding, and retuning your family and life, you should remember this great promise as well.

The Lord your God is with you, He is mighty to save. He will take great delight in you, He will quiet you with His love, He will rejoice over you with singing (Zeph. 3:17). Start here, and soon you will discover there are many more.

ENDNOTES

1. Max Lucado, *When God Whispers Your Name* (Word Publishing, Dallas, TX, 1994), p. 81.
2. Johannes P. Louw and Eugene A. Nida, Editors, *Dictionary of Biblical Languages With Semantic Domains*: Hebrew (Old Testament): 1215 (United Bible Societies, New York, NY,), p. 42.

Praying Scripture assures us that we are consistently praying the will and Word of God over our lives.

CHAPTER TWO

Blessing Your Home and Family

When I talk with people about blessing a home and a family, I notice consistent patterns of misunderstanding. People rarely know what blessing actually is, and because of that they find it difficult to pray and speak blessings effectively.

> *When you enter the home, give it your blessing. If it turns out to be a worthy home, let your blessing stand.*
> MATT. 10:12,13A NLT

The Bible reveals what a blessing is. It also reveals how to bless, who has the authority and responsibility to bless, and what the benefits of blessing are. My prayer is that you will clearly understand the benefits of blessing your family and home, and that God will motivate you to bless your family through prayer.

In his book *Hope for the Troubled* Heart, Billy Graham reminds us, "Heaven is full of answers to prayer for which no one bothered to ask."[1] This is one of our biggest problems. We do not have answers and fulfillment because we do not ask for them (Note: Jas. 4:2). God loves to pour out His blessings on His children who ask. I want you to have the ability and the confidence to pray blessings over your family and your home.

It is impossible to overstate the importance of praying God's blessing on your family and home. Dr. David Jeremiah writes, "Prayer does not come naturally to any of us. In our more honest moments, we all admit that it is a struggle to pray as we'd like. And yet there is no avoiding the fact that Scripture insists God has hard-wired the universe in such a way that He works primarily through prayer. No doubt He could have chosen some other method, but He has chosen to do most of His work through prayer. In some ways, He has made Himself subservient to the prayers of His people. And certainly He has conditioned a good portion of His BLESSING upon our willingness to pray."[2]

> IT IS IMPOSSIBLE TO OVERSTATE THE IMPORTANCE OF PRAYING GOD'S BLESSING ON YOUR FAMILY AND HOME.

When God named the Temple, He said, "*My house will be called a house of prayer for all nations*" (Isa. 56:7). Notice that God did not say His house would be called a "House of Socializing," or of "Political Action Committees," or of "Good Deeds." These things may be good; but they are not God's central goal for us. His desire is for us to engage in prayer, aided by the Holy Spirit. Jesus reiterated this not long before He was crucified. Profiteers (money-changers) had set up shop in the temple and were hindering prayer. With righteous anger, Jesus drove them out, declaring the same words God spoke through Isaiah (Note: Jn. 2:12-25; Matt. 21:12-21). God is passionate about His house being a house of prayer, and He wants your home to be a house of prayer as well.

THE BIBLICAL DEFINITION OF BLESSING

Blessing is an empowered word, proclaimed to convey a richer, fuller, and more abundant life. It is a gift bestowed by God to establish happiness. In the Old Testament, a blessing was part of a father's inheritance to his children. Blessings were pronounced by a priest regarding the bounty of harvest and the prosperity of a household (Note: Ezek. 44:30). A blessing was declared over the Temple where God's presence was to reside (Note: 1 Kgs. 8:14-53). In fact, throughout Scripture, God's promises of blessing are abundant.

By New Testament times, blessing included all the gifts promised through Jesus. The Bible puts it like this: "Every good and perfect gift is from above, coming down from the Father of the heavenly lights, who does not change like shifting shadows" (Jas. 1:17). Everything that is positive, encouraging, uplifting, good, wholesome, and healthy comes from God as an expression of His love and blessing.

I consulted the *Brown, Driver, Briggs, Gesenius Lexicon of the Old Testament* to find out just how the Old Testament writers used the word bless. Bless comes from the Hebrew word *barach* or *barak* (baw-rak); meaning, "To bless; to salute, congratulate, thank, praise; to kneel down." *Barach* is the root word from which *baruch* ("blessed one") and *barachah* ("blessing") are derived. *Berech*, "knee," is the root of "bless."

In the Old Testament, one got down on his knees when preparing to speak or receive words of blessing, whether to God in heaven or to the king on his throne. Kneeling down to pray, even today, is an act of honor, indicating the importance of God's right to rule one's life. The word *barak* is found 289 times in the Old Testament. Obviously the Lord is interested in blessings.[3]

God the Creator's initial communication to His newly created man and woman was to bless them with a mandate to have the dominate role in creation (Note: Gen. 1:28). Thus, blessing is an intrinsic part of God's desire regarding His creation. Jack Hayford writes that to bless is "the act of declaring, or extending-through-pronouncement, God's favor and goodness upon others. The significance in a righteously administered blessing is not only the good effect of words upon the hearer, but in the fact that the Holy Spirit will endow the words with the power to bring them to pass."[4] And *Nelson's New Illustrated Bible Dictionary* offers this definition: "The act of declaring, or wishing, favor and goodness upon others. God also blesses people by giving life, riches, fruitfulness, or plenty[5] (Note: Gen. 1:22, 28). His greatest blessings are to turn us from evil (Note: Acts 3:25,26) and the forgiveness of our sins (Note: Rom. 4:7,8)."

Blessing is an established component of both the Old Testament and the New Testament:

- In the Bible, God blesses His people when He gives them gifts, both physical and spiritual (Note: Gen. 1:22; 24:35; Job 42:12; Ps. 45:2; 104:24, 35).

- Parents sent their children to be with Jesus, but His disciples dismissed them. Jesus rebuked the disciples and told the children to come to Him. Then He blessed each one (Note: Mk. 10:13-16).

- Believers in Jesus can bless one another by expressing good wishes or offering prayers to God for other people's well being (Note: Gen. 24:60; 31:55; 1 Sam. 2:20).

- Fathers and mothers blessed their children (Heb. 11:20), and grandparents blessed their grandchildren (Note: Heb. 11:21; Prov. 8:21).

It is thrilling to read that the act of blessing children by parents and grandparents is included in God's "Hall of Faith" (Note: Heb. 11). This passage lists some of the greatest stories of the Bible: Moses leaving Egypt, David conquering kingdoms, Sarah having a child in her old age, and others. It also speaks of the multitude of unknowns who conquered their challenges by faith.

Isaac and Jacob are remembered by the blessings they pronounced over their children and grandchildren as much as any other aspect of their lives. Think about that. Blessing children and grandchildren is just as important to God—just as much an act of faith—as building the ark was for Noah (Note: Heb. 11:7).

Our Biblical Mandate to Bless

As spiritual heirs of Abraham, God gives us the privilege, responsibility, and authority to bless others (Note: Gen. 12:1-3; Rom. 4:13-16; Gal. 3:26-29).

In Genesis 12, He made this promise to Abraham:

> *Leave your country, your people and your father's household and go to the land I will show you.*

> *I will make you into a great nation and I will bless you; I will make your name great, and you will be a blessing. I will bless those who bless you, and whoever curses you I will curse; and all peoples on earth will be blessed through you.*
>
> GEN. 12:1-3

As New Testament believers, we are the spiritual seed of Abraham, and the promises to Him were given to us:

> *You are all sons of God through faith in Christ Jesus, for all of you who were baptized into Christ have clothed yourselves with Christ. There is neither Jew nor Greek, slave nor free, male nor female, for you are all one in Christ Jesus. If you belong to Christ, then you are Abraham's seed, and heirs according to the promise.*
>
> GAL. 3:26-29

If you put your faith in Jesus, you are "an heir according to the promise" (Note: Gal. 3:29). In fact, seven times in Romans chapter 4, Abraham is called our father, as a prototype of all believers everywhere in every generation. It was not through the Law that Abraham and his offspring received the promise. It was through the righteousness that comes by faith. The promise comes by faith so that it may be by grace and thus be guaranteed to all Abraham's offspring—not only to those who are of the Law, but also to those who

> IF YOU PUT YOUR FAITH IN JESUS, YOU ARE "AN HEIR ACCORDING TO THE PROMISE."

are of the faith of Abraham. He is the father of us all. (Note: Rom. 4:13-16).

In Genesis, Abraham blessed Isaac, Isaac blessed Jacob, and Jacob blessed his twelve sons. In fact, blessing continues throughout all of Scripture. But notice how God's blessing came to Abraham.

> *I will surely bless you and make your descendants as numerous as the stars in the sky and as the sand on the seashore.*
> GEN. 22:17

The implication is that what God promised to Abraham, He promised to us as His spiritual seed. Therefore, we are heirs, inheritors of all the blessings given to Abraham. Again, I refer to Jack Hayford's writing to expand this point.

> Through Abraham, whom He wills to become "a great nation" (restoring rule) and to whom He chooses to give a "great name" (restoring authority), God declares His plans to beget innumerable children who will be modeled after this prototypical "father of faith." This truth is confirmed in Romans 4:13, where Abraham's designation as "heir of the world" parallels Jesus' promise that His followers, who humble themselves in faith, shall also be recipients of "the kingdom" and shall "inherit the earth"[6] (Note: Matt. 5:3-5).

God's Ways of Blessing

It is clear in Scripture that the concept of blessing is much greater than the mere implication of happiness or the adding of value to lives. When you bless someone, you speak goodness into their life. God promised to bless His people in countless ways and circumstances if we would follow Him and His desires. Deuteronomy 28 offers us a comprehensive list of ways God wants to bless His people.

- Blessed shall you be in the city, and blessed shall you be in the country (our location).

- Blessed shall be the fruit of your body (our children), the produce of your ground, and the increase of your herds (our vocation).

- Blessed shall be your basket and your kneading bowl (our supply).

- You will be blessed when you come in and blessed when you go out (our everyday activities).

- The Lord will grant that the enemies who rise up against you will be defeated before you.

- They will come at you from one direction but flee from you in seven (our victory in conflict).

- The Lord will send a blessing on your barns and on everything you put your hand to (our work).

- The Lord your God will bless you in the land He is giving you (our abundant provision for everything we need).

Common Myths About Blessing

It is important to have a clear understanding of the significance of blessing, and particularly the importance of blessing your home, your family, and others as well. Yet, many people are hindered from being effective in praying and speaking blessings because of these commonly held myths. Here are four of the most common ones.

MYTH #1: ONLY A PASTOR, PRIEST, OR MINISTER CAN BLESS MY HOME

Not true! Though it is good to have a Christian leader bless your home and family, it is not a necessity. As a believer, God has qualified you to ask and speak His blessing over your family. God has ordained, empowered, and qualified every believer to bless their home, their food, their children, and one another. We have all been made priests unto our God (Note: 1 Pet. 2:9,10).

> GOD HAS QUALIFIED YOU TO ASK AND SPEAK HIS BLESSING OVER YOUR FAMILY.

> *[Jesus] has made us to be a kingdom and priests to serve His God and Father—to Him be glory and power forever and ever! Amen.*
> REV. 1:6, BRACKETS ADDED

God wants to use you to speak His power and blessing over your family and home.

MYTH #2: IF I BLESS MY HOME, NOTHING BAD WILL HAPPEN TO MY FAMILY OR ME

This is a widely held opinion, but actually it is a myth. A prayer of blessing is not a magic incantation that keeps all evil away from you. We live in a fallen world and bad things happen. They happen to those who walk with the Lord as well as those who do not, exept with God situations change (Note: Matt. 5:45). Inviting God's blessing is not a charm or a mystical chant to be dragged out like a talisman or a lucky rabbit's foot. The truth from God's Word is that He will work all things (and He means all things) together for our good and for His glory, even things we consider to be bad (Note: Rom. 8:28). Life brings many circumstances that are not what we desire. However, if we allow Him to, God will work everything out for our good. He promises to always give us a way out. The circumstance you face may be a purifying fire, so be patient, let God do His work. Wait for His perfect timing and see Him bring about the better than you imagined blessing.

> *No temptation has seized you except what is common to man. And God is faithful; He will not let you be tempted beyond what you can bear. But when you are tempted, He will also provide a way out so that you can stand up under it.*
>
> 1 COR. 10:13

During those times of difficulty and strain, it is important to remember and understand God's ways.

> *"For My thoughts are not your thoughts, neither are your ways My ways," declares the Lord.*
>
> *"As the heavens are higher than the earth; so are My ways higher than your ways and My thoughts than your thoughts."*
>
> ISA. 55:8-9

MYTH #3: IF I BLESS MY HOME, GOD WILL CANCEL OUT THE CONSEQUENCES OF BAD DECISIONS AND ACTIONS I MADE PRIOR TO SPEAKING THE BLESSING

Actions have consequences, always. Bad decisions usually lead to unpleasant consequences, in spite of the miraculous testimony you may have heard that someone was delivered without them. Those are exceptions, not guarantees. Quite frankly, God often uses the results of our decisions as teaching tools to help us become purified and grow in our Christian walk (Note: 1 Pet. 1:7; Jas. 1:2-5). On some rare occasions, God may choose to spare us from the most obvious consequences of our decisions or actions. However, the biblical principle is that we reap what we sow.

> ***Do not be deceived: God cannot be mocked.***
> ***A man reaps what he sows.***
>
> GAL. 6:7

This verse is not negative. It is an encouragement, a positive promise that if you start to bless your family and home now, good results will come from those seeds of life you speak out loud in and to your family.

MYTH #4: BECAUSE WE ARE A CHRISTIAN FAMILY, GOD'S BLESSING IS AUTOMATIC

God's blessings are never automatic. It is true that the Lord lives in every believer (Note: Col. 1:27). However, His grace, power, and presence come into the homes and hearts in which He is invited in a special way. God will make Himself at home in the heart of every family member who specifically asks Him.

> *Ask and it will be given to you; seek and you will find; knock and the door will be opened to you.*
> MATT. 7:7

When we ask the Lord to bless us by entering our homes, we are requesting that He make Himself completely at home in our homes, in our hearts, and in our lives. Then Christ will make His home in your heart as you trust in Him. Your roots will grow down into God's love and keep you strong (Note: Eph. 3:17, NLT).

As we go further in our journey, you must understand this: blessing your family and home is not a one-time act that guarantees uninterrupted protection. Blessing your family and home needs to become a way of life, an intentional pursuit that keeps you close to the heart of God. This book is designed to assist you in developing a consistent habit of asking for the Lord's blessing and protection throughout the day, every day.

> BLESSING YOUR HOME AND FAMILY NEEDS TO BECOME A WAY OF LIFE.

ENDNOTES

1. Billy Graham, *Hope For the Troubled Heart* (Word Publishing: Waco, TX, 1991), p. 171.
2. David Jeremiah, *Prayer: The Great Adventure* (Multnomah Publishers: Sisters, OR,1997), 35 (emphasis added).
3. Brown, Driver, Briggs, and Gesenius, *Hebrew and English Lexicon with an Appendix containing the Biblical Aramaic*, (Hendrickson Publishers, Peabody, MA, 1985).
4. Jack W. Hayford and Thomas Nelson Publishers, *Hayford's Bible Handbook* (Nashville: Thomas Nelson Publishers, 1995).
5. Ronald F. Youngblood, F. F. Bruce, R. K. Harrison and Thomas Nelson Publishers, *Nelson's New Illustrated Bible Dictionary*, Rev. Ed. of: Nelson's Illustrated Bible Dictionary.; Includes Index. (Nashville: T. Nelson, 1995).
6. Jack W. Hayford and Thomas Nelson Publishers, *Hayford's Bible Handbook* (Nashville: Thomas Nelson Publishers, 1995).

Christ will make
His home in your
heart as you
trust in Him.

CHAPTER THREE

Praying Through Your Home With Scripture

PRAYING SCRIPTURE

For years I did not understand the importance of including Scripture in my prayers. After all, God is fully aware of what He said and what was written. Why should I remind Him of His words? As I studied the Bible and meditated on its application to my life, I realized how important it is to rehearse God's promises. They don't remind Him of His words—rather, they embrace His Words as living promises we have been given. Thus, I will offer you seven biblical reasons why we should pray Scripture.

1. **Jesus is our model of a prayer filled life.** As such, He consistently invoked Scripture as a way to resist temptation (Note: Matt. 4:1-11; Lk. 4:1-13). He answered His critics with Scripture rather than intellectual arguments (Note: Matt. 12:5; 19:4). He even prayed the words of the Psalms from the cross (Note: Lk. 23:46; Mk. 15:34). A prayer life which is fortified with Scripture has a much better grasp on the heart of the Father.

2. **Praying Scripture offers a defense against error, and an offensive weapon against the onslaught of the enemy.** Praying God's Word utilizes the two-edged sword of the Bible to establish truth and to resist deceit. *"Take the . . . sword of the Spirit, which is the word of God"* (Note: Eph. 6:17). *"For the word of God is living and active. Sharper than any double-edged sword"* (Heb. 4:12). When your family is under spiritual attack and is going through difficult times, you wield the sword of the spirit by praying God's Word, in the power of the Holy Spirit (not your own power). This builds a defense for your family, establishing truth in your home. And when God calls you to a new level, praying God's Word in the power of the Spirit advances you as you confront opposing forces.

3. **Praying God's Word builds your faith.** Praying specific promises found in Scripture, particularly as you declare them out loud, builds your own faith. *"So then faith comes by hearing, and hearing by the word of God"* (Rom. 10:17 NKJV).

4. **Rehearsing Scripture as prayer is an echo of God's voice.** It brings assurance that you are praying the mind and will of God for whatever request you are placing before Him, thus you can approach His throne of grace with confidence (Note: Heb.

4:14-16). *"This is the confidence we have in approaching God: that if we ask anything according to His will, He hears us. And if we know that He hears us—whatever we ask—we know that we have what we asked of Him"* (1 Jn. 5:14-15).

5. **Praying God's Word invites God's power into your prayer requests.** *"For with God nothing is ever impossible, and no word from God shall be without power or impossible of fulfillment"* (Lk. 1:37 AMP).

6. **Proclaiming the promises and declarations of Scripture in prayer coordinates prayer agreement for increased power.** When you pray together with other believers in accordance with His will, you find greater strength. *"Five of you will chase a hundred, and a hundred of you will chase ten thousand, and your enemies will fall by the sword before you"* (Lev. 26:8). God tells us, *"Again, I tell you that if two of you on earth agree about anything you ask for, it will be done for you by my Father in heaven"* (Matt. 18:19). *"Though one may be overpowered, two can defend themselves. A cord of three strands is not quickly broken"* (Eccl. 4:12).

7. **In praying a promise from God's Word, you focus on Him because only He can fulfill the promise.** Ask Him whose desire is to make us more like Jesus (Note: Rom. 8:29), to help you focus on the God who made the promise. We are to fix our gaze on God, and glance at our requests for blessing. God will bless with incredible answers that are beyond all we could ask or imagine (Note: Eph. 3:20).

It is not hard for prayers to unconsciously drift over into self-centeredness. We all have needs and desires, and knowing God wants to bless us, we try to reach beyond His Provision. God has promised to fulfill every promise [He has made] to us, if we abide in Him (Note: Jn. 15:4-7).

Praying verses from the Bible assures us that we are praying consistently with the will and Word of God, rather than imposing wishes on our lives that God will not approve. Furthermore, blessing others by praying God's Word anticipates the outcome to our prayers, elevating our confidence, both in God, and in our walk with Him. Ultimately, praying the Word of God is a way of saturating your life with a God-enhanced view of all things.

> PRAYING FROM THE BIBLE ASSURES US THAT WE ARE PRAYING CONSISTENTLY WITH THE WILL AND WORD OF GOD.

Beth Moore writes in her book *Praying God's Word*:

> God has handed us two sticks of dynamite with which to demolish our stronghold: His Word and prayer. What is more powerful than two sticks of dynamite placed in separate locations? Two strapped together . . . taking two sticks of dynamite—prayer and the Word—strapping them together, and igniting them with faith in what God says He can do. Hallelujah!

To hear His Word sprinkled like seasoning throughout our prayers is surely pleasing to God, because His Word reflects His desires. To hear them spoken aloud *"And we are confident that He hears us whenever we ask for anything that pleases Him. And since we know He hears us when* we make our requests, we also know that He will give us what we ask for" (1 Jn. 5:14,15 NLT).

> ***All Scripture is God-breathed and is useful for teaching, rebuking, correcting and training in righteousness, so that the man of God may be thoroughly equipped for every good work.***
>
> 2 TIM. 3:16,17

> ***For everything that was written in the past was written to teach us, so that through endurance and the encouragement of the Scriptures we might have hope.***
>
> ROM. 15:4

> ***Above all, you must understand that no prophecy of Scripture came about by the prophet's own interpretation. For prophecy never had its origin in the will of man, but men spoke from God as they were carried along by the Holy Spirit.***
>
> 2 PET. 1:20,21

Prayer Walking Your Home and Its Surroundings

Over quite a number of years, Christians have followed a practice of walking around a specific geographical area, praying and proclaiming God's promises as they went. After being delivered from Egypt, God instructed His people to walk into the Promised Land as He commanded, and *"every place on which the sole of your foot treads shall be yours"* (Deut. 11:24). And to Joshua, He repeated the fulfillment of that promise (Note: Josh. 1:3). Hence, we connect the practice of praying and walking through specific areas in proclaiming God's blessings and appropriating God's promises.

Chapter four of this book begins a detailed, guided course of action for prayer walking through your home and blessing your family, your household, and your own life as well. God has entrusted you with the property in which you dwell, whether you own it, rent it, or occupy it through someone else's kindness. The responsibility for its maintenance and cleanliness are yours. The provision it offers for shelter and comfort are yours as well. Taking a purposeful journey from room to room and through the surrounding landscape is in your best interests and those of your family as well.

The prayers I have recorded are my own. I have repeated them again and again as I have gone through my own dwelling, proclaiming and releasing God's blessings aloud over my home, my family, and those who pass within these walls. I encourage you to read them aloud as you pass through the various rooms of your home. Rewrite them as you discover your own pace, but carefully and specifically pray in each instance which applies to your family.

In some cases, you will find prayers which may not apply. Those are for someone else. Find the ones which apply to your circumstances and use them until you become confident in forming your own. It is not improper to repeat the prayers someone else has written if you are being sincere and honest. Those prayers have genuine influence on your family, your home, and you. As your heart embraces the power and blessing of prayer walking through your home, you will see how important and effective this exercise can be.

With my whole heart I join you in asking God to bless you, your family, and your home. I ask the God of all grace to cleanse every part, covering you and yours with the precious blood of His Son, Jesus—the protective covering of His covenant love. I pray also that He will fill you with His Holy Spirit, refreshing you with His presence each day.

Begin your walk with the cleansing prayer (pg. 174). Then proceed to the outside of your home. Pray over the land (pg. 32), then the foundation (pg. 42), then the roof (pg. 49). Next, enter through the front door and proceed room by room, following the pattern presented in the book (chapters 5-8). You do not need to concern yourself with rooms that are not in your home. But, you will need to pray over each space. If there are more than one of a specific area, repeat the process for each of those rooms. Some of the prayers are for people, not rooms. When you pray, do so over each one individually, and all of them collectively.

Praying God's word utilizes the two-edged sword of the Bible to establish truth and to resist deceit.

CHAPTER FOUR

Your Property and Surroundings

ANOINTING THE LAND

It is important to understand, your dwelling is more than your living quarters. It takes in the property which surrounds your home. You are responsible for its maintenance and security, as well as its use for times of enjoyment and beautification. You should prayer walk your land, anointing and dedicating it for God's use in His desired way. Anoint with oil (or water if oil is not available), praying while dripping the liquid on the ground as you walk the perimeter of your property and building. You may also rub the anointing substance on doors, fences, and walls.

By anointing your property, you are marking it, delineating, creating a boundary and declaring the Lord's dominion—that whatever happens there will be consistent with His will and glorify Him. Anoint the land, pray that the Holy Spirit will permeate it and remove everything that is not from God. As you walk, pray for the Lord's protection as well. Scripture tells us, *"And the yoke will be destroyed because of the anointing oil"* (Isa. 10:27, NKJV). If you live in a condominium or an apartment complex, anoint the outside of the building, the door(s), the lobby, the elevators and stairs—wherever you or your loved ones may find themselves. Ask the Lord to protect your family and home with His guardian angels (Note: Heb. 1:7).

You should also pray over other things; objects you might find outside your home which influence your thoughts and feelings. For your convenience, an alphabetical list of such objects is provided in the Appendix of this book (beginning on pg. 177). You might begin with prayers for: Birds, Buildings/Structures, Bushes/Trees/Plants, Cars, City Skyline, Doors, Fences/Gates, Flags, Flowers, Grass, Locks/Security/Protection, Rivers/Streams, Roads, Rocks, Walls, Sky, and Water.

Prayer Over the Land

Thank You, Lord, for the beauty of this land and of Your creation. Thank You that every good and perfect gift comes from above and is from You. I love You for Your creativity, the diversity of Your creation, and the amazing way Your genius is on display every day through Your creation of nature.

Lord, You created the land. You made it. You maintain it, and I am simply passing by for a period of time on this earth. You have graciously allowed me to use this property during my time here. I am committing this land and building to You, heavenly Father, for Your use and for Your glory.

Lord, I am trusting You to use my space as You intend. I ask for Your blessing, Your protection, and Your direction in knowing how to use this land and building in the most effective ways to bring You glory. I pray that my intended uses will be for godly purposes and if they are not, I ask You to reveal those things that displease You, Lord. If anyone is misusing this property, convict them to change their hearts and behavior or cause them to leave it immediately because this property is to be dedicated for use for Your purposes only.

Father, in walking the perimeter of this property and anointing this land, praying and dedicating it to You, I am reminded of how Your people walked around Jericho until You gave them a victory over their enemies. I ask for greater faith, to trust You as I wait for unanswered prayers to be answered, and commit to obeying Your voice immediately when I understand what You want me to do. Just as You caused the walls of Jericho to collapse (Note: Josh. 6:20), I ask that You bring down any problem walls within this family. Father, do Your will in this house and on this land. Help me to remember the great victories You have given our family and will give our family in the future.

Just as God's people consistently used physical objects to remind them of spiritual victories He had given them, you may set up memorial stones on the land (Note: Gen. 28:11; Ex. 28:12; Neh. 2:20; Acts 10:4). Memorial stones are literal rocks or stones you place somewhere in your yard so that when you see them, you will remember the way God supplied your family's need at a specific point in time. You could also use a spiritual marker, which might be several rocks resting on top of each other, as a reminder of a special spiritual day in your family that you would like to commemorate. This might be when a family member comes to know the Lord or is baptized. Perhaps you will want to write out some Scriptures and then bury them under the rock. Either that, or write them on the rock. Soon you will have a memorial stone garden.

As you do this, you can pray:

> Bless me and my family now as we remember the wonderful ways You have blessed us with significant spiritual victories. Lord, we set a physical reminder, a memorial stone, and anoint it to be a constant reminder of Your grace and mercy in our lives (Note: Josh. 4:4-7).
>
> I ask for protection for my family and friends who are here. In Your Word, You give this promise, *"The Lord will protect him and preserve his life; He will bless him in the land"* (Ps. 41:2). I ask for Your protective covering to be on every person who

enters this land and building. You have given authority to me, as the caretaker of this land and building, thus, I command any and everything which does not please You to be removed from this land immediately. In Jesus' name, amen.

Now you can continue praying over specific items using the individual prayers listed in the Appendix (pg. 177).

SCRIPTURE REFERENCES REGARDING PRAYER OVER YOUR HOME AND PROPERTY

- *"Every good and perfect gift is from above, coming down from the Father of heavenly lights, who does not change like shifting shadows"* (Jas. 1:17, NIV).

- *"So whether you eat or drink or whatever you do, do it all for the glory of God"* (1 Cor. 10:31).

- *"In the land the Lord your God is giving you to possess as your inheritance, He will richly bless you"* (Deut. 15:4).

- *"The Lord's curse is on the house of the wicked, but He blesses the home of the righteous"* (Prov. 3:33).

- *"For I will pour water on the thirsty land, and streams on the dry ground; I will pour out my Spirit on your offspring, and my blessing on your descendants. They will spring up like grass in a meadow, like poplar trees by flowing streams"* (Isa. 4:3-4).

- *"The grass withers and the flowers fall, but the Word of our God endures forever"* (Isa. 40:8).

> ⚘ *"'No weapon forged against you will prevail, and you will refute every tongue that accuses you. This is the heritage of the servants of the Lord, and this is their vindication from me,' declares the Lord"* (Isa. 54:17).

THE FOUNDATION

As you begin your prayer walk through your home, you must start with the foundation. This is extremely important because without a solid foundation, your house will literally fall apart. The foundation is invisible, concealed from sight. But if your foundation is weak, your house is at risk. The same can be said for your family's spiritual foundation.

Several years ago, my family purchased a house in order to remodel it into our dream home. Almost immediately we discovered there were huge cracks in the foundation. To renovate the house in this condition would have been an utter waste. We were forced to rebuild from the ground up. Termites had eaten away the wood just above the foundation and the house had been built over a hidden spring, a sure recipe for disaster. The house looked fantastic on the outside but it was seriously compromised on the inside, below the surface. The damage was hidden, but it made the house unlivable.

REBUILDING REQUIRED

In order to rebuild, before we could even pour footings for a new foundation, we had to dig deep into the ground and add solid fill dirt. This fill had to be packed down carefully in a very specific way. Only after the ground was prepared properly could we lay a new foundation and begin the work of reconstruction. It was exhausting work which took several months, but eventually, with a square and level foundation, we could build securely.

There are hidden areas within us that only the Holy Spirit can reach. Only He can pack the soil of our hearts in the correct way to support the strong foundation of our faith. Our part is to surrender our selfish wills to Him, give up our rights to self-direction, and allow Him access into the deep places of our souls. Without this work of the Holy Spirit, we will not have the sound foundation on which to build healthy individual lives. And without healthy individual spiritual lives, we cannot effectively build strong foundations for our families.

> THERE ARE HIDDEN AREAS WITHIN US THAT ONLY THE HOLY SPIRIT CAN REACH

THE IMPORTANCE OF A STRONG FOUNDATION

A foundation determines the size, strength, longevity, and overall health of a building or house. It governs how long a structure will be able to stand securely. It must be designed to carry the full weight of the completed structure, or it will eventually fail and the structure will fall. The same thing is true in a family home. The foundation on which your family is built will determine the strength, and overall health of your family home. It will also determine the spiritual longevity for future generations: your children, grandchildren, and great-grandchildren.

In order to lay a foundation for a healthy, wholesome, loving, and godly family, you constantly need to turn to the Lord. It is important to listen to people with understanding of God's Word, people who have wisdom and a spirit of prayer. Skilled architects and experienced craftsmen are necessary when building physical buildings. How much more important is having people who are skilled in prayer and God's Word as part of your life? These are people you can turn to for encouragement, wisdom, and direction when you need it. They become partners with you in prayer, which is essential to building your own house of prayer.

When the old foundation is flawed, laying a new, solid foundation is a two-step process: removing the old and building the new. First, remove the faulty foundations. Only then can you build a solid, healthy, enduring one. This is actually the process God uses to:

- build our lives personally (Note: Matt. 7:24-27);

- build our families (Note: Ps. 127:1-2);

- build a nation (Note: Jer. 1:9-10).

The apostle Paul knew the importance of a sound foundation in building a life that would bring glory to God. He wrote in his letter to the church at Corinth:

> *For no one can lay any foundation other than the one already laid, which is Jesus Christ. If anyone builds on this foundation using gold, silver, costly stones, wood, hay or straw, their work will be shown for what it is, because the day will bring it to light. It will be revealed with fire, and the fire will test the quality of each person's work. If what has been built survives, the builder will receive a reward.*

> *If it is burned up, the builder will suffer loss but yet will be saved—even though only as one escaping through the flames.*
> 1 COR. 3:11-15

Jesus Christ is the only sure foundation on which a life can be built. If we start constructing our lives on anything else, we are actually setting ourselves up for disaster. Striving to remodel your life on your own without being sure your foundation will endure is a waste of energy. Are you doing that? Will your future be secure when the storms of life hit?

If you have been building on weak or false foundations, you must be willing to tear them down and start all over. It may be hard, but in the end it will be worth the effort. Faulty foundations often crumble under the pressures of life. Self-gratifying information found in the latest self-help books may not really help. Relying on your own abilities—"if I just work harder…" gets you in trouble. And an elevated sense of self-assurance—"I'm doing okay, I don't need God's help …" is a sure way to ultimate defeat.

> IF YOU HAVE BEEN BUILDING ON WEAK OR FALSE FOUNDATIONS, YOU MUST BE WILLING TO TEAR THEM DOWN AND START ALL OVER.

Perhaps the weakness in your foundation is not very obvious. Perhaps the cracks are being overlooked altogether. You should ask yourself some questions before you go much further, just to be confident you are on a solid footing.

Are there small fissures that will lead to huge cracks in the foundation of your life or in your family relationships? Are frequent episodes of anger or passive-aggressive behaviors in your home causing underlying tension? Are you and your family merely hoping everything will turn out all right, instead of actively building on God's foundation for your lives? Honest answers to questions like this and aggressive responses to resolve such issues, will determine the strength of your foundations in the future.

WHO IS YOUR ARCHITECT/BUILDER?

The architectural plans for a house or a building are the guidelines for construction. They determine where to place the load-bearing walls. They govern the size and placement of its rooms and floors. They also outline where the electrical wiring and the plumbing are to be placed. An architect designs the structure and drafts blueprints of the design. A skilled builder constructs the house according to the plan. Until the house is completed, the architect and builder are in charge and make sure the plans are carried out correctly. They are the authority directing the construction of the building.

How could someone discover the real authority in your life? If they watched you make decisions and you never ask the Lord for direction, what could they conclude? Every decision we make is based on some source of authority following some plan. God is, or should be, the architect and builder of your life. Is He your source of authority? Do you trust the plans He has made for you? Or, are you regarding Him more as an add-on while you rely on your own ideas and plans?

DO YOU TRUST THE PLANS GOD HAS MADE FOR YOU?

Open yourself up to the very real possibility that God has a better, brighter future for you and your family than you have ever imagined. You can replace a faulty foundation with a lasting, stable base. Disjointed, unstable families can become firmly grounded, healthy, and whole.

Emotionally treacherous homes, filled with conflict or chaos can become safe shelters against life's storms. Homes devastated by the loss of love, connectedness, and warmth can once again be places of laughter, love, and joy. And homes that are quite healthy can become even stronger.

Dear friend, my deepest desire in putting these thoughts on paper is to encourage you in your own life and family journey. I want to strengthen your hope that you can be a blessing to your home and family, even to your extended family and friends. But the key to all of this is a firm foundation.

Repairing a family home begins when at least one person becomes willing to pray and keep praying. Is God nudging you to be that person? Is He asking you to believe Him and be personally repaired first, beginning with the foundation of your own heart? Don't imagine you have to come up with a plan to rebuild your whole family. Life's too short to labor in vain (Note: Ps. 127:1). Be sure that your one true foundation is Jesus Christ. It is He who was crucified, died, and was buried. On the third day, He rose again. Build your life and the lives of your family on this profession of faith.

Now, let's pray God's richest blessings on the foundation of your home.

Foundation Prayer

Lord, I thank You that Your Word directly addresses foundations. You say that when we put Your words into practice, it "*...is like a man building a house, who dug down deep and laid the foundation on rock. When a flood came, the torrent struck that house but could not shake it, because it was well built. But the one who hears my words and does not put them into practice is like a man who built a house on the ground without a foundation. The moment the torrent struck the house, it collapsed, and its destruction was complete*" (Lk. 6:47-49).

Lord, I thank You, as the Creator and Foundation of our lives (Note: 1 Sam. 2:8b) "*for everything in the universe. I praise You as my all-powerful Source for life. You, Lord, have promised protection to me and to my family*" (Ps. 91:1-3. personalized). Because I am building on You as my firm foundation, I will not be afraid of any storm that threatens my life, nor will I be discouraged because of any struggles my family may face.

I know "*the battle is not mine but Yours, Lord*" (1 Sam. 17:47, personalized). You have promised to be my Protector and Deliverer. I love you, Lord; you are my strength. "*You, Lord are my rock, my fortress, and my savior; You, my God are my rock, in whom I find protection. You are my shield, the power that saves me, and my place of safety"* (Ps. 18:1-2, personalized). You have told me I do not need to fight any battles on my own. Instead, I will rely on You as my firm foundation and praise You for the victory You are bringing to me (2 Chron. 20:1-8).

Thank You that You are delivering me from every enemy (Note: Ps. 18:48) that would seek to undermine the foundation and faith I have in You—enemies like discouragement, fear, loss, disappointment, failure, negativity, devastating change, or ___*(fill in the blank)*___. I do not want to take one step or move in any direction away from You as my solid Rock and my Deliverer (Note: Ps. 144:2). Thank You no matter where I have been or what I have done, no matter what has happened in the past, You are my Foundation, and I am choosing to build my life on You. You have promised to meet me where I am in life—physically, mentally, emotionally, and spiritually. Give me wisdom in building a lasting and satisfying life with You (Note: 1 Cor. 1:18-22). Thank You I do not have to fear rejection or shame. You accept me just as I am and assure me I do not have to fear condemnation (Note: Rom. 8:1).

Lord, please show me where my faults and faulty thinking lay so I may submit to them being torn down and then built back up again. I know You will only give me good things, because good only comes from You.

Wherever the foundation our family has built on is cracked and flawed, I know it will not withstand the storms that inevitably will come our way. Be merciful to us and tear down any plans which have not been built on You. I know this will mean some pain in the present, but joy will come. I want my life and the life of my family to be built on You and Your values alone. Forgive us for any place where we have built upon any false foundations. We now want to be set on the foundation of Jesus Christ, the everlasting Son of God.

Lord, I pray this prayer You love to answer: *"Search me, O God, and know my heart; test me and know my anxious thoughts. Point out anything in me that offends you, and lead me along the path of everlasting life"* (Ps. 139:23-24 NLT, personalized). Show me anything offensive to You and give me the courage and grace to change. Where I am following Your will for my life, encourage me in the path of everlasting life.

Bless our home's foundation which we now present to You, O God. *"This one thing I ask of You—the thing I seek most—to live in the house of the Lord all the days of my life, delighting in the Your perfections and meditating in Your Temple. For You will conceal me there when troubles come; You will hide me in Your sanctuary. You will place me out of reach on a high rock*" (Ps. 27:4-5 NLT, personalized). In Jesus' name, amen.

- **Note**: As you pray God's blessing on your foundation, go into your basement and look at the foundation walls. Walk around the outside of your home if it is built on a slab of concrete. Even if you live in a building without a visible foundation, you can still anoint the base of the outside walls of the building. If you live in a multi-storied building, you should still anoint the foundation. Whatever your circumstances dictate, it is of the greatest importance to begin by praying for your family's foundation, so don't skip this section.

SCRIPTURE VERSES REGARDING FOUNDATIONS

- *"My own hand laid the foundations of the earth, and my right hand spread out the heavens; when I summon them, they all stand up together"* (Isa. 48:13).

- *"He raises the poor from the dust and lifts the needy from the ash heap; He seats them with princes and has them inherit a throne of honor. For the foundations of the earth are the Lord's; on them He has set the world"* (1 Sam. 2:8).

- *"He will be the sure foundation for your times, a rich store of salvation and wisdom and knowledge; the fear of the Lord is the key to this treasure"* (Isa. 33:6).

- *"As for everyone who comes to me and hears my words and puts them into practice, I will show you what they are like. They are like a man building a house, who dug down deep and laid the foundation on rock. When a flood came, the torrent struck that house but could not shake it, because it was well built"* (Lk. 6:47-48).

- *"No one can lay any foundation other than the one already laid, which is Jesus Christ"* (1 Cor. 3:11).

- God's solid foundation stands firm, sealed with this inscription: *"The Lord knows those who are His,"* and, *"Everyone who confesses the name of the Lord must turn away from wickedness"* (2 Tim. 2:19).

THE ROOF

A roof provides protection from the elements—the rains of spring, the harsh sun of summer, the snow of winter. But the roof of a house is more than an umbrella over our family and our possessions; it also gives the house its unique shape and design, even more so than the exterior walls. The roof improves or impairs the environment within, the heating and cooling of the home. A roof can be designed to transfer most of its weight load to the outside walls, thus taking the pressure off the interior walls. There is much more to the roof than meets the eye.

Many roofs are made from trusses which are three-sided wooden structures. Each side works with the other two, and no individual side is more important than another. Such trusses mirror the three-fold nature of God, who is identified as the Trinity. God is three unique Persons: Father, Son, and Holy Spirit. Yet God is uniquely One in

Himself. There is no separating God the Father from God the Son or God the Holy Spirit although each one has a distinct role.

When Jesus died on the cross, His blood was shed, the very blood of God Himself. This blood is our covering—it covers (deals with), or forgives our sin. It is our covering of protection from those elements of the world that would seek to harm us and take us away from our loving Father. There is no power greater than the blood of Jesus and the name of Jesus. In the same way as a physical roof covers our house, the blood of Jesus is our home's covering. One of the beautiful metaphors of Scripture describes this covering. The psalmist says it like this: *"He will cover you with His feathers. He will shelter you with His wings. His faithful promises are your armor and protection"* (Ps. 91:4 NLT). The covering of Jesus' blood is like the sheltering wings of an eagle or a hen, protecting its young from the elements of a storm. Thus, He protects us from life's storms and the blazing heat of daily trials.

> THERE IS NO POWER GREATER THAN THE BLOOD OF JESUS AND THE NAME OF JESUS.

THE TEN COMMANDMENTS AS A COVERING

In addition to Jesus' blood covering of protection, the Lord has given us specific protection for our lives as individuals and as a family. We find this in the book of Exodus. It recounts how Moses led the Israelites out of slavery in Egypt. The journey was to take them to a land of God's promise, but first God set some things in order. He called Moses to the top of a mountain and gave him specific laws or ways to live. These were to ensure the Israelites would stay on the right course with God, and not only the Israelites. These laws are important for everyone. We know them as the Ten Commandments (Note: Ex. 20:1-21).

No one, except Jesus, has ever perfectly observed these decrees, not even the heroes of the Bible. But, they have been the moral standard, both of the Hebrew religion and of Christianity. It is important to know Jesus fulfilled the requirements of the law through His life, death, and resurrection. He gave us a pardon from the consequences of our sins which we receive by accepting Him as Savior and Lord. We then begin a life in which Jesus is living in and through us. But the Ten Commandments are still morally pure, and they are important for our lives. They provide a very sound roof over our spiritual lives under which we can find protection as we rely on the blood and name of Jesus. We no longer look to our own strength to live the way God instructs us to live. Instead, we cooperate with Him and the Holy Spirit, living according to His commands, and finding forgiveness and cleansing when we fail (Note: 1 Jn. 1:9).

Jesus was asked which one was the greatest commandment. His surprising answer was a summarization of the first five of these commandments. He said,

> *"You shall love the Lord your God with all your heart, with all your soul, and with all your mind. This is the first and greatest commandment."*
> MATT. 22:36-40, NKJV

Then, He summarized the next five as He went on to say:

> *"And the second is like it: 'You shall love your neighbor as yourself. On these two commandments hang all the Law and the Prophets.'"*

It has been said that every law in society is a practical application of one of the Ten Commandments.

As you ask God's blessing on the roof of your home, use it as an opportunity to invite God to help you live by the Ten Commandments in your life and your family's lives. Ask His blessing as a protective covering from the unpredictable elements that can damage your spiritual home.

ROOF PRAYERS

With my voice, I speak to you, O Lord, asking You to keep our family's home and roof secure and covered with Your protection. I ask You, Lord, to be our protective covering for our home, like You said, *"… everyone who hears these words of Mine and puts them into practice is like a wise man who built his house on the rock. The rain came down, the streams rose, and the winds blew and beat against that house; yet it did not fall, because it had its foundation on the rock."*

"But everyone who hears these words of Mine and does not put them into practice is like a foolish man who built his house on sand. The rain came down, the streams rose, and the winds blew

and beat against that house, and it fell with a great crash" (Matt. 7:24-27). Protect us from any physical or spiritual forces of destruction.

I want a life that is pleasing to You, from bottom to top, in our family, from the solidity of our foundation to the protection of our roof and all that is in between. I know we cannot fulfill Your law in our own strength or power. I trust You, Holy Spirit, to live through us, guiding us in all our ways so that we may please You. I treasure You and Your Ten Commandments as a way to have a sound roof over our family.

Lord, You are our only unmoving, protective covering from the world (Note: Ps. 91). Just as our building's roof protects us from storms, we will be protected as we live according to Your timeless commandments. *Your great and precious promises to my family and me will never be broken"* (2 Pet. 1:3-4, personalized), and we will always be secure in You (Note: Ps. 18:1-2). Cover us with the blood of Jesus wherever we are.

I speak these prayers aloud, verbalizing my commitment to live all of life, for as long as You grant me life, in harmony with Your Ten Commandments. I ask the same for my family, my extended family, my loved ones, and my prayer partners. Thank You that You have placed Your Holy Spirit in my soul to lead and guide me in all of Your ways. Thank You that You don't leave me to myself to try to fulfill these commandments. I will trust You, oh Lord, to be my strength and my help in my day of trouble.

Lord, as I anoint this roof, I ask for the blessing of your covering, on the roof of my home, and on my family. In Jesus' name, amen.

- **Note**: If you cannot physically reach your roof to anoint it, you can touch a rain spout or some other area that touches your roof or top floor instead. If this is not practical, extend your hand toward the roof.

THE TEN COMMANDMENTS IN THE OLD AND NEW TESTAMENTS

1. *"You shall have no other gods before Me"* (Ex. 20:3 NKJV).

    I will put You first in my life and accept no substitutes for my relationship with You. I will have no other god before You (Note: Ex. 20:1,2; Acts 14:15; Jn. 4:21-23; 1 Tim. 2:5; Jas. 2:19; 1 Cor. 8:6).

2. *"You shall not make for yourself a carved image—any likeness of anything that is in heaven above, or that is in the earth beneath, or that is in the water under the earth; you shall not bow down to them nor serve them"* (Ex. 20:4-5a NKJV).

I will not make any images of You because no image is worthy of You as the Lord of the universe. You are God, and You desire worshippers who are sincere, honest, and truthful (Note: Ex. 20:3; Acts 17:29; Rom. 1:22,23; 1 Jn. 5:21; 1 Cor. 10:7,14).

3. *"You shall not take the name of the Lord your God in vain, for the Lord will not hold him guiltless who takes His name in vain"* (Ex. 20:7).

I will strive to take You seriously as evidenced by not speaking Your name in a vain, empty manner (Note: Ex. 20:5-7; Jas. 5:12; Matt. 5:33-37; 6:5-9).

4. *"Remember the Sabbath day, to keep it holy ... For in six days the Lord made the heavens and the earth, the sea, and all that is in them, and rested the seventh day. Therefore the Lord blessed the Sabbath day and hallowed it"* (Ex. 20:8,11 KJV).

I will remember to rest and not constantly work, play, shop, or be too busy. I will remember to reserve the Sabbath as a special day for You, Lord (Note: Ex. 20:8-11).

5. ***"Honor your father and your mother, that your days may be long upon the land which the Lord your God is giving you"*** (Ex. 20:12 NKJV).

   I will honor the parents You have given me as evidenced by obeying them when I am in their home as a child (Note: Eph. 6:1-3) and providing for them when they are older (Note: Matt. 15:1-9). Help me to remember they are my earthly parents—only humans subject to having many faults—but You are my always faithful, always loving Heavenly Father (Note: Ex. 20:12; Eph. 6:1-4; Matt. 15:1-9).

6. ***"You shall not murder"*** (Ex. 20:13 NKJV).

   I will strive to do whatever I can to protect and celebrate the lives of others. I will not murder anyone physically, in my heart, with my tongue, or in my thoughts by hating them, resenting them, or holding bitterness (Note: Ex. 20:13; 1 Jn. 3:15; Matt. 5:21-22).

7. ***"You shall not commit adultery"*** (Ex. 20:14 NKJV).

   I will cherish, honor, and love my spouse above all others by protecting my marriage from any form of adultery—physical or emotional (Note: Matt. 5:27-30). Help me to put my spouse's needs first and to respect my marriage covenant. (Note: Ex. 20:14; Matt. 5:27,28; 1 Cor. 5:1-13, 6:9-20; Heb. 13:4).

8. ***"You shall not steal"*** (Ex. 20:15 NKJV).

> I will not steal from another person (Note: Ex. 20:15; Eph. 4:28; 2 Thess. 3:10-12; Jas. 5:1-4).

9. ***"You shall not bear false witness against your neighbor"*** (Ex. 20:16 NKJV).

> I am committed to speaking the truth in love, so I will not bear false testimony (lie) against another person. I will strive to always speak the truth in love (Note: Ex. 20:16; Col. 3:9; Eph. 4:25) seeking the Holy Spirit's help first.

10. ***"You shall not covet ... anything that is your neighbor's"*** (Ex. 20:17 NKJV).

> I am committed to be content with who I am and what You have given me. I commit to not covet anyone or anything that does not belong to me. Father, I ask You to remove any jealousy in my heart and replace it with love (Note: Ex. 20:17; Eph. 5:3; Lk. 12:15-21).

ADDITIONAL SCRIPTURES

> *"One thing I ask from the Lord, this only do I seek: that I may dwell in the house of the Lord all the days of my life, to gaze on the beauty of the Lord and to seek Him in His temple. For in the*

day of trouble He will keep me safe in His dwelling; He will hide me in the shelter of His sacred tent and set me high upon a rock" (Ps. 27:4-5).

- "How abundant are the good things that You have stored up for those who fear You, that You bestow in the sight of all, on those who take refuge in You. In the shelter of Your presence You hide them from all human intrigues; You keep them safe in Your dwelling from accusing tongues" (Ps. 31:19-20).

- "I long to dwell in Your tent forever and take refuge in the shelter of Your wings" (Ps. 61:4).

- "Whoever dwells in the shelter of the Most High will rest in the shadow of the Almighty. I will say of the Lord, 'He is my refuge and my fortress, my God, in whom I trust'" (Ps. 91:1-2).

- "I have given you authority to trample on snakes and scorpions and to overcome all the power of the enemy; nothing will harm you" (Lk. 10:19).

- "Do not repay evil with evil or insult with insult. Instead, repay evil with blessing so that you may inherit a blessing" (1 Pet. 3:9).

I WANT MY LIFE AND THE LIFE OF MY FAMILY TO BE BUILT ON YOU AND YOUR VALUES ALONE. FORGIVE US FOR ANY PLACE WHERE WE HAVE BUILT A FALSE FOUNDATION.

CHAPTER FIVE

Common Rooms and Living Spaces

THE ENTRANCE

The entry into your house is more than just a door. It is a vital point of introducing family, friends, and strangers into your home. Whether it is a specific room, a small hallway, or simply a door that opens into the dwelling, it determines whether you, your family, and your guests will experience comfort, safety, and happiness while they are in your home. Unlike other doors that may lead in or out of your house, the entry offers a way to protect our families from dangers that might enter. It is a kind of screening area where we evaluate each visitor before they are allowed access to the rest of the house. Only family and close friends have access through other doors.

What do people notice when they cross your threshold for the first time? Do they see the well-worn mat that says welcome, or hear the musical sound of a doorbell? Do they notice the scratches on the door trim, engraved by moving things that didn't quite fit in and out? Would their first glance say God lives here? Would they feel comfortable, sensing they could belong here with you?

By praying this blessing of God regarding your entrance, you are asking Him to bring godly intentions, attitudes, and behaviors into your home. You are also asking Him to help you discern when to close the door to the enemy. If the front door to your home were left open all the time, any person or animal could enter and gain access to every room in the home.

Only a fool leaves the front door wide open. Wise folks know when to shut the door to bad influences and when to open it to godly influences. Be conscious that you should ask the Lord to reveal any negative influences entering your home or any object that detracts from the presence of the Lord in your home.

Entry Prayer

Lord, I open the door of our home to You and invite You to enter in. Ensure this will be a place where Your Holy Spirit dwells. May all who enter through this door sense Your presence, and may Your blessing rest upon them as long as they are here. Though many will walk through this door with great burdens, let them hear Your call to *"come to Me all you who are weary and burdened, and I will give you rest"* (Matt. 11:28). Let their worries disappear.

Lord, grant to every person who enters our door, an immediate and strong sense that our home is different because You live here. God, we embrace Your values, Your wisdom, Your strength, Your Word, and Your love (Note: Eph. 3:14-21). Before we even say a word, cause our home to reflect You.

I ask Your blessing on the feet of those who cross this threshold. I pray each one entering our family home will feel Jesus' love and be completely at home. I ask Your blessing on the arms of those who walk through these doors that they will be open and receptive to Your Holy Spirit working in their lives (Note: Jn. 16:13-17). I ask Your blessing on those who enter here, that their minds and actions would be transformed. Bless the eyes of those who enter that they may see You. Give them ears to hear what You would say to them. Soften the ones whose hearts are hardened or emotionally shut down, and lighten the load of those who are burdened or sad, so they would trust You completely.

Father, I also ask You bless our visitors and family as they depart through this door. Let Your peace continue to rest on everyone who leaves our house. This is both an entrance into our home and an entrance into the world outside of our home. You are Lord over all—both in and out of our home. We know You can be with us wherever we are. Bless everyone, as they come in and go out through this entrance. In Jesus' name, amen.

Remember, you should consult the list of prayers over individual objects in your entryway. I would recommend using the prayers for: Art, Chairs, Doors, Draperies/Window Coverings, Floors, Locks/Security/Protection, Keys, Plants, Shoes, and Stairs/Steps (See: Appendix).

ADDITIONAL SCRIPTURES

- *"I am the gate. Those who come in through me will be saved. They will come and go freely and will find good pastures"* (Jn. 10:9 NLT).

- *"When you enter, you will come to a secure people with a spacious land; for God has given it into your hand, a place where there is no lack of anything that is on the earth"* (Jdg. 18:10 NASB).

- *"But as for me, by Your abundant lovingkindness I will enter Your house, At Your holy temple I will bow in reverence for You"* (Ps. 5:7 NASB).

- *"I long, yes, I faint with longing to enter the courts of the Lord. With my whole being, body and soul, I will shout joyfully to the living God"* (Ps. 84:2 NLT).

- *"Not everyone who calls out to me, 'Lord! Lord!' will enter the Kingdom of Heaven. Only those who actually do the will of my Father in heaven will enter"* (Matt. 7:21 NLT).

The Family Room

What immediately springs to mind when you think of your family room? Do you remember setting up your first family room? You wanted it to be comfortable and welcoming, a place where friends and family could make themselves at home.

When I look around my family room, I reflect on the many activities and laughter that have happened here. Many family gatherings, kid parties, and sleepovers have been enjoyed in our family room. Kids have watched television and movies, played cards and board games, practiced musical instruments, and studied for tests. They have entertained old and new friends, hosted school friends for group projects, and just hung out.

Family rooms are places where we can enjoy time together. We communicate, laugh together, cry together, share what is on our hearts, and spend time together. Much of the time we experience closeness as a family not by what we are saying or doing, but just by being together, sharing our space with one another. Does your family room provide an atmosphere where it is easy to relax with others? So much of life is not found in the doing but in the being.

> WE EXPERIENCE CLOSENESS AS A FAMILY NOT BY WHAT WE ARE SAYING OR DOING, BUT JUST BY BEING TOGETHER.

If there is strife in the family? The family room is the place it will be most apparent. When you enter the family room, does your child leave? Is there coldness in the air in the family room? If that is the case, the family room is the area in which you most need the Lord's presence. God loves to heal and restore relationships.

> *The law of the Lord is perfect, restoring the soul. The statutes of the Lord are trustworthy, making wise the simple.*
>
> PS. 19:7

If you have ever experienced the pain of a strained relationship or had a child stray from the faith, remember God knows what it's like to have a difficult relationship. Consider this: *"The son of Seth, the son of Adam, the son of God"* (Lk. 3:38) The first man, Adam, is called *"the son of God"* in this verse, and he was the first rebellious child. God pursued Adam—and pursues us—with a passion just as you do with someone you love if they are going astray.

A passionate pursuit of God can mend relationships between siblings who seem to be at a tragic impasse. Jacob and Esau were twin brothers, the sons of Isaac and Rebekah. They couldn't have been more different. As the firstborn, Esau was entitled to be blessed by their father, but he sold that right to his brother Jacob in return for something to eat. Jacob had to trick their father in order to obtain the blessing, but when he did, Esau was not happy. In fact, Esau threatened to kill his brother (Gen. 27:41).

Jacob ran for his life, and during that separation, God used the time apart to bless both Jacob and Esau with prosperity and family. The time eventually came for the two brothers to meet again, and Jacob was sure he was going to have to beg for his life or at the least try to pay off his brother. But when the two finally came face-to-face, Esau threw his arms around Jacob and welcomed him (Note: Gen. 33:4).

I encourage you to passionately pursue your relationships and kids in prayer. Ask God to restore and heal the troubled areas in your life. You will be amazed at God's shocking and elaborate plan to reconcile your family in a way far better than you can ever imagine and bring your children home to the warmth of the family. You will be amazed at what God can do; *"for nothing is impossible with God"* (Lk. 1:37).

While praying for your family room, take some time to reflect on ways God is making it a room where the sense of family can be tangibly felt, where acceptance, encouragement, and—above all—love are evident.

FAMILY ROOM PRAYERS

Lord, when I gather with my family and friends, I pray You would fill this room with Your presence. Saturate this room with Your Holy Spirit so all we say and do gives You glory. In Jesus' name, I ask You, Holy Spirit, to envelop each person who comes into our family room with love, mercy, and grace.

Lord, I ask You be present in every conversation. I ask You to *"set a guard over our mouths, O Lord; keep watch over the doors of our lips"* (Ps. 141:3, personalized). I ask that *You* silence us when we are speaking things other than what You intend for us to say. We want Your thoughts to enter our minds and fill our mouths because You tell us *"don't use foul or abusive language. Let everything you say be good and helpful, so that your words will be an encouragement to those who hear them"* (Eph. 4:29 NLT).

I ask You to guide us, to lead our conversations with love, joy, peace, patience, kindness, goodness, faithfulness, gentleness, and self-control, which are the fruit of the Spirit. You have promised we will bear these traits if we follow You and Your teachings (Note: Gal. 5:22-23).

As we discuss events in our lives, let us do so prayerfully, determining that You are to be glorified in all we say. Instead of critical spirits, Lord, I ask You form in us spirits of love, forgiveness, patience, and kindness. Give us wisdom to see the world the way You see it. Show us where You want us to work with You. Let us listen closely to where You want our conversations to go, and not to overlook our divine appointments.

As we decide which media to use, from television to movies to music, direct us to only select things You find acceptable. Let our choices be uplifting, positive, and appropriate, so we, Your children, will cautiously participate in pure, holy entertainment. I pray that if an inappropriate choice is made by someone else, with provocative sexuality, vulgar innuendo, cursing, violence, terror or hate, we would have the courage to speak up and redirect the programming. Remind us of Your desires for us to "*... be careful to live a blameless life—when You* *will come to help me? ... to lead lives of integrity in our own home. ... to refuse to look at anything vile and vulgar"* (Ps. 101:2-3 NLT, personalized) and, *"to test everything, to hold on to the good, and to avoid every kind of evil"* (1 Thess. 5:21-22, personalized).

Lord, You desire our family and everyone in this family room to look, think, and act like You and to be consistent with Your will in our lives. As was said of Abraham, Your servant, may it *be* said of my family, *"I have singled him (her) out so that he (she) will direct his (her) sons and their families to keep the way of the Lord by doing what is right and just. Then I will do for___(your name)___ all that I have promised* (Gen. 18:19 NLT, personalized*).*

I ask if we are having a Bible study in this room, You will fill it with Your Holy Spirit's presence. Guide, guard, and direct the conversations so they are pleasing to You and foster a spirit of unity. I ask a special blessing on all the people participating in studying the Bible here, that their minds will absorb Your truth (Note: Jn. 17:17), and they will experience the grace that comes from Your Word (See: Acts 20:32). Open eyes, ears, and hearts to Your wisdom and love.

I pray as the children do homework or work on projects, they will put forth only their best effort, and cooperatively work together. Remind them to work diligently and cheerfully at whatever they do, just as though they were working for the Lord rather than for people (Note: Col. 3:23 NLT). Help my children act in a way that is pleasing to You, Lord, because You say, *"even children are known by the way they act, whether their conduct is pure, and whether it is right"* (Prov. 20:11 NLT).

I pray You will help and encourage my children to have wholesome attitudes and generous, loving spirits toward their friends who visit. Shield us from negativity, gossip, lying, slander, or abusive speech that could come out of their mouths while they are in this family room (Note: Col. 3:5-9). I pray my children will connect with friends in an excellent way, one that will encourage strong friendships for life rather than building shallow relationships around superficial speech. I ask for wisdom for my children in choosing good friends with whom they can connect and mutually encourage one another in right living because You remind us that, *"Bad company corrupts good character"* (1 Cor. 15:33 NLT).

Lord, I pray as my children play board games, video games, or *(fill in the blank with a favorite activity in your family room)*, they will embrace fair play with a good attitude, having fun, without demeaning or treating others badly. I pray they would have good relationships and an edifying time for everyone playing the game. I pray as my children mature and abandon small children's games, they will also mature in every area of their lives in this room, just as You did when You became a mature man in wisdom, and stature, and in favor with God and man (Note: Lk. 2:52).

Lord, as my children practice their musical instruments, I pray they will enjoy their time and find it to be soothing and uplifting. You remind us in Your Word to train ourselves to be godly (Note: 1 Tim. 4:7), so help my children understand that discipline and training in music will help them to discipline themselves for godliness as well.

Lord, as I look at the books on my shelves, I am reminded that my thinking needs to be consistent with Your precepts and commands in the Bible. I pray You will place within my heart a deep desire to know and understand You more as I read and study Your Word. I want to read only books that are pleasing to You. Give me a clear mind, a teachable spirit, and the ability to learn. You have said, *"But grow in the grace and knowledge of our Lord and Savior Jesus Christ. To Him be glory both now and forever! Amen"* (2 Pet. 3:18). I especially pray You will open the eyes of my heart to focus on You, because You have promised, You will keep me in perfect peace because I trust in you, and my thoughts are fixed on you (Isa. 26:3 NLT, personalized).

Lord, I pray Your blessing on my family room now. I invite You to make Yourself completely at home in this room, in every room of our home and to be the leader of our home. In Jesus' name, amen.

When you begin to pray over the items and furniture in your family room, I recommend using the prayers for the following objects: Chairs, Chess Set/Board Games, Computers, Draperies/Window Coverings, Fans, Fireplaces, Floors, Footstools, Globe/Map, Lamps (Lights), Mirrors, Pets, Phones, Sofas, Stairs/Steps, Stereo/CD Player/iPod™, Television/DVD Player, Toys, and Work Desks (See: Appendix).

ADDITIONAL SCRIPTURES

- *"The ark of God remained with the family of Obed-Edom in his house for three months, and the Lord blessed his household and everything he had"* (1 Chron. 13:14).

- *"Now fear the Lord and serve Him with all faithfulness. Throw away the gods your ancestors worshiped beyond the Euphrates River and in Egypt, and serve the Lord. But if serving the Lord seems undesirable to you, then choose for yourselves this day whom you will serve, whether the gods your ancestors served beyond the Euphrates, or the gods of the Amorites, in whose land you are* living. But as for me and my household, we will serve the Lord" (Josh. 24:14,15).

- "You are no longer foreigners and strangers, but fellow citizens with God's people and also members of His household, built on the foundation of the apostles and prophets, with Christ Jesus Himself as the chief cornerstone" (Eph. 2:19,20).

- "Every kingdom divided against itself will be ruined, and every city or household divided against itself will not stand" (Matt. 12:25).

KITCHEN AND DINING ROOM PRAYERS

In many homes today, the kitchen is the crossroads of activity, and quite often it is a hub for family communication. Mine certainly is. At times it is an exciting and joyful place to be. At others, it is emotional or confrontational. But life consistently happens here.

My kitchen is in a continual state of activity—especially for my teenagers and their friends. After all, that is where the food is, and everyone eats. Often, when family members are seeking snacks or drinks, spontaneous conversation breaks out. That sometimes leads to something much deeper. More than a few times my children have described conversations they had in school and how they had felt about them. I discovered significant decisions they had made which would have had far-reaching implications. As I listen I pray silently about those decisions, knowing God will answer my prayer. I also pray for a strong bond with each child, a bond only God can develop. Thus, more than physical food is prepared in the kitchen of your home.

Food is a major theme in God's Word, both physical food and spiritual food. Thus, a recipe offers a useful comparison of how God is at work to make our lives complete and full. Notice the ingredients that go into making your favorite meal. By themselves, some of these are quite tasty, but many of them taste horrible—flour, vinegar, oil, baking soda, etc. When those items are mixed together, however, they make a delicious, wonderfully satisfying meal.

This is what the Lord does in our lives and in our family home. God mixes all of our different life experiences together, both good and bad, to create a wonderful, well balanced, satisfying life. *And we know that God causes everything to work together for the good of those who love God and are called according to His purpose for them* (Rom. 8:28 NLT).

Sometimes, God uses our natural physical craving for food or drink to redirect our focus to spiritual realities. We do grow hungry. We seek to end that hunger by partaking of food we find in the kitchen. But, our Lord knows what we need goes beyond physical food, and He reminds us that our physical hunger is a reminder of a greater, spiritual reality. He alone is the Bread of Life who gives lasting fulfillment (Note: Jn. 6:35-51). When we are thirsty and long for a drink of cold water on a hot day, He reminds us that He is the One who quenches our deeper thirst. *"As the deer pants for streams of water, so my soul pants for You, O God. My soul thirsts for God, for the living God. When can I go and meet with God?"* (Ps. 42:1-2)

> SOMETIMES, GOD USES OUR NATURAL PHYSICAL CRAVING FOR FOOD OR DRINK TO REDIRECT OUR FOCUS TO SPIRITUAL REALITIES.

May God bless you, my friend, and every person who passes through your kitchen, to eat, to converse, to fellowship, or simply to unload a burden. May He use our physical appetites as reminders that He alone satisfies our deepest desires.

KITCHEN/EATING AREA PRAYER

Lord, please help me to include time for my children during my prep time in the kitchen. If they come in and want to talk about their day, remind me to stop, to look lovingly into their eyes with a smile as I listen intently to every word. Please continuously open our communication with each other, developing a deeper, closer relationship. Help me offer godly advice, appropriate to their situation, because You say: *"A word aptly spoken is like apples of gold in settings of silver"* (Prov. 25:11).

Help me include all of my family members in the preparation of the food for our family. It is a time for sharing ideas to open communication channels. Lord, help us to speak genuine, loving words, and participate in loving actions to one another—using good manners and speaking with a gracious tone of voice while we eat together.

Lord, keep me thinking clearly about the value of nutrition as I plan our meals each day, so that my family will live life to its fullest potential. May I be ever mindful of the need to go back to the basics in cooking for my family and decrease any dependence on fast-food meals.

Lord, as I serve my spouse, children, extended family and friends, and as I learn their needs from each day, may my love abound still more in real knowledge and all discernment (Note: Phil. 1:9-11). As I plan and prepare meals, may each meal be created because of my love for You and gratefulness for the gifts You have given my family (Note: Jas. 1:17), so that when I see Christ someday, I can say confidently that I did everything without complaining or arguing (Note: Phil. 2:14). As I invest my time, heart, and life in prayer when I am in this kitchen, I believe that arguments will decrease. Warm my heart toward my spouse, my children, or _(fill in the blank with someone with whom you may need reconciliation)_ . May there be abundant fruit of Your Spirit—Your love, joy, peace, patience, kindness, gentleness, faithfulness, goodness and self-control (Note: Gal. 5:22 NLT)—which will yield understanding, cheerfulness, patience, helpfulness, and calm in my kitchen.

Lord Jesus, our immediate family, extended family, and friends will be sitting at my kitchen table enjoying a meal with us regularly and on special occasions. (You may wish to anoint each chair with oil as you pray this part of the prayer.) I pray over this chair where *(fill in the name of the person)* usually sits for meals. I pray for physical health to be established through the food that is eaten. I pray for peace and rest as they sit at this table.

We pray that if there is any uneasiness in the heart of anyone who joins us that it will be melted away by good food, refreshing drinks, and interesting conversation around our table. I pray that everyone who eats at our table will feel a sincere happiness and a sense of Your peace and presence because You say, *"Never will I leave you, no never will I forsake you"* (Heb. 13:5). May Your blessing be on every person who sits at our kitchen table and chairs, Jehovah Ra'ah (the Lord my Shepherd).

Let there be laughter and joy as we gather. Let there be freedom to share hurts and needs as we meet as a family. Help us to be good listeners as others share what is on their minds and hearts. Let us honor each other's vulnerability, establishing this table as a safe place to share thoughts, ideas, desires, hurts, and problems.

I invite You to be the invisible Guest at every meal; to be the honored Lord as we give You thanks for every part of our meal—for the chairs, the table, the plates, the silverware, the glasses, the food and drink, the decorations, and for each one who sits at this table. *"You prepare a table before me"* (Ps. 23:5).

Abundant Lord, Provider of all good things, I thank You that You supply for all of us and all of Your creation:. *"These all look to You to give them their food at the proper time. When You give it to them, they gather it up; when You open Your hand, they are satisfied with good things"* (Ps. 104:27-28). Lord, I thank You for supplying our every need.

Just as finishing a wonderful meal satisfies the body and makes us feel happy and full, please make our hearts glad and full as well. Lord Jesus, we invite You to saturate our lives with Your love and grace: *"When Your words came, I ate them; they were my joy and my heart's delight, for I bear Your name, O Lord God Almighty"* (Jer. 15:16). Just as a recipe may call for kneading the dough, I pray that You will knead into my family's hearts everything that is pleasing to You.

Help us to be genuinely grateful for all You have provided for us. Father, I ask You to bless this kitchen, the food, its consumption, and all who enter it. Thank You that You know exactly which ingredients to mix into our lives at just the right time to make us more like Your Son, Jesus Christ. May Your will be done in our lives. In Jesus' name, amen.

For individual prayers for your kitchen and dining room, I recommend: Chairs, Clocks, Doors, Floors, Flowers, Food, Plants, Plates/Dishes, Positive Words/Messages, Stereo/CD Player/iPod™, Table, Vessels/Vases, and Water. (See: Appendix).

ADDITIONAL SCRIPTURES

- *"I will refresh the weary and satisfy the faint"* (Jer. 31:25).

- *"You will be like a well-watered garden, like a spring whose waters never fail"* (Isa. 58:11).

- *"He humbled you, causing you to hunger and then feeding you with manna, which neither you nor your fathers had known, to teach you that man does not live on bread alone but on every word that comes from the mouth of the Lord"* (Deut. 8:3).

- *"Jesus declared, 'I am the bread of life. He who comes to me will never go hungry, and he who believes in me will never be thirsty'"* (Jn. 6:32-35).

- *"Jesus answered, 'Everyone who drinks this water will be thirsty again, but whoever drinks the water I give him will never thirst. Indeed, the water I give him will become in him a spring of water welling up to eternal life'"* (Jn. 4:13-14).

- *"Let them give thanks to the Lord for His unfailing love and His wonderful deeds for men, for He satisfies the thirsty and fills the hungry with good things"* (Ps. 107:8-9).

- *"He makes grass grow for the cattle, and plants for man to cultivate—bringing forth food from the earth ... bread that sustains his heart"* (Ps. 104:14-27).

- *"May God himself, the God of peace, sanctify you through and through. May your whole spirit, soul and body be kept blameless at the coming of our Lord Jesus Christ"* (1 Thess. 5:23).

- *"Do you not know that your body is a temple of the Holy Spirit, who is in you, whom you have received from God? You are not your own; you were bought at a price. Therefore honor God with your body"* (1 Cor. 6:19-20).

- *"For God did not give us a spirit of timidity, but a spirit of power, of love and of self- discipline"* (2 Tim. 1:6-7).

- *"The eyes of all look to you, and you give them their food at the proper time"* (Ps. 145:15).

- *"He upholds the cause of the oppressed and gives food to the hungry. The Lord sets prisoners free"* (Ps. 146:7).

- *"She is like the merchant ships, bringing her food from afar. She gets up while it is still dark; she provides food for her family and portions for her servant girls"* (Prov. 31:14-15).

- *"Come, all you who are thirsty, come to the waters; and you who have no money, come, buy and eat! Come, buy wine and milk without money and without cost. Why spend money on what is not bread, and your labor on what does not satisfy? Listen, listen to me, and eat what is good, and your soul will delight in the richest of fare. Give ear and come to me; hear me, that your soul may live. I will make an everlasting covenant with you, my faithful love promised to David"* (Isa. 55:1-3).

- *"Taste and see that the Lord is good; blessed is the man who takes refuge in Him"* (Ps. 34:8).

- "He provides food for those who fear Him; He remembers His covenant forever"(Ps. 111:5).

- "Therefore I tell you, do not worry about your life, what you will eat or drink; or about your body, what you will wear. Is not life more important than food, and the body more important than clothes?" (Matt. 6:25).

- "But He said to them, 'I have food to eat that you know nothing about.' Then His disciples said to each other, 'Could someone have brought him food?' 'My food,' said Jesus, 'is to do the will of Him who sent me and to finish His work'" (Jn. 4:32-34).

- "They feast on the abundance of your house; You give them drink from your river of delights" (Ps. 36:8).

A PASSIONATE PURSUIT
OF GOD CAN MEND
RELATIONSHIPS BETWEEN
FAMILY MEMBERS.

CHAPTER SIX

Sleeping and Personal Areas

Master Bedroom

Whether you're greeting the promise of a new day or saying goodbye to a particularly difficult one, you usually find yourself in your master bedroom. More than any other room in your home, this is your personal space—yours and if you are married, your spouse's space also. There is something reassuring about settling in for a good night's sleep. Free from the distractions of the day, you can grow quiet. You can have meaningful discussions with your spouse about most anything that is on your mind. The emotional intimacy and shared unity such moments bring cannot be overestimated. They absolutely enhance the success of a marriage.

While the physical relationship is fundamentally important, it is not the basis of true intimacy. Loving, honorable communication is. Of course, physical intimacy is its own kind of communication and the master bedroom offers privacy for this. It also provides a secluded place to talk, rest, relax, or just be together—especially important in the over-scheduled, ever-busy world we inhabit. Carving out time to be alone together on a consistent basis, even if it's at the end of the day, is particularly fulfilling in marriage. Such conversations bring a stability to decision making and balance to schedules.

The master bedroom also offers a sheltered place for prayer. We read in the Gospels that Jesus would draw away to a secluded place for prayer. Just imagine—God's Son needed to pray. He would walk up into a mountain glen, or stride off into the wilderness of the desert. There He would find His own personal sanctuary to commune with the Father. If Jesus found it necessary to find solitude so He could focus in prayer, how much more do we need to do so ourselves?

Why not do that right at home in the master bedroom? Having time alone to pray and focus on the Lord can rejuvenate you for the tasks facing you the rest of the day.

As you prepare for the day, you can also prepare your heart and mind, allowing the quietness of your master bedroom to surround you. It is during this time that the thoughts and ideas which will carry us through the day begin to take shape. Worried concerns can be entrusted to the One who knows how our day will end, even before it begins. Ambitious plans can be submitted to His guidance before careless decisions are made. How you dress your heart and mind is at least as important as how you dress your body. Your life is so much more than the clothing you wear and the way you look.

I have written several prayers below. You can use these words as a template for praying over your master bedroom. You should add specific prayers about areas of concern (something we see modeled in numerous Psalms). This section also offers prayers which address several variations of marital status or situations, areas which may or may not pertain to your particular situation.

However, they do apply to someone. If that is you, understand that God's love sets us free and covers us in grace.

It's important to begin prayer for the bedrooms—whether you are married, single, divorced or widowed, with repentance, asking the Lord to forgive and cleanse before blessing. You can insert this cleansing prayer:

> Lord, I ask You to cleanse me, the master bedroom, and these objects from anything or any activity that has taken place here which is dishonoring or displeasing to You. Bring to my memory anything I may have knowledge of or unknowingly participated in that was against Your wishes, Lord. I ask forgiveness on behalf of me and my ancestors. I repent and renounce any alliance with these unacceptable practices and I align myself only with You, Father God, and Jesus.

Dear friend, I encourage you to pray God's blessing for your marriage and for your master bedroom. As you pray over the individual objects in your master bedroom, I recommend: Activity Calendar, Bed/Sheets/Pillows, Blankets, Books/Reading Material, Clocks, Colors, Computers, Doors, Draperies/Window Coverings, Floors, Flowers,

Footstools, Lamps (Lights), Shoes, Stereo/CD Player/iPod™, and Television/DVD Player. (See: Appendix).

Prayer for Couples.

Father, giver of every good gift, I pray that __(*spouse or future spouse*)__ and I will experience oneness in spirit, soul, heart, mind, and body. Grant us a calm spirit, peace in our hearts individually and as a couple, and agape love at the core of our being today and in our relationship with one another and with You. We will hear many voices today, Abba Father, and I pray we will hear Your voice above all others. Fill us to overflowing with Your Holy Spirit, and remove everything in us that is not pleasing to You.

We pray for balance today in our bodies, our souls, our spirits, and in our schedules and the time we give each other (Note: 1 Thess. 5:23). Show us how to convince each other of our love, and help us to be able demonstrate our love to each other in ways we each understand.

Lord, You tell us that You have called us to peace (Note: 1 Cor. 7:15). When we have disagreements, help us to settle our differences in peaceful, considerate ways. When we are asked questions which need attention, but we are busy or distracted by other things, remind us to answer peacefully, not in a way that causes strife.

Lord, I pray You would establish and sustain bonds of love between *(spouse's name)* and me that cannot be broken. Show us how to love in ever-deepening, respectful ways we clearly perceive. Instill in us mutual respect and admiration for each other, so we become and remain the greatest of friends, uncompromising supporters, and verbal vocal champions (Note: Eph. 5:18-21). Give us time together—just the two of us— to engage in activities that strengthen our bonds of love and trust. Where our love has diminished, been lost, destroyed, or buried under a burden of disappointment, restore our hearts with deep and honest desire. Give us the strength to hold on to the good in our marriage, especially during times when one of us doesn't feel like loving the other. Help us to imitate Your love during those difficult times, Lord, and choose to respond lovingly and not in the way we feel. You loved us in such a way that You gave Your only Son, so help us make the choice to give unconditional love to each other (Note: Jn. 3:16). Help us refrain from selfishness—self-seeking and self-serving in our marriage—and enable us to live for the benefit of the other.

Lord, I want to please You by loving my spouse. Teach me how to love my spouse in a clear, understandable love language with Your kind of love—love that is patient and kind; love that is not jealous or boastful nor proud or rude; that does not demand its own way (Note: 1 Cor. 13:4-6). Teach me how to pray for my spouse as You are constantly praying for me (Note: Heb. 4:14-16). May my love be a sweet, fragrant gift to You. Show me how to wash [my spouse] with the water of Your Word (Note: Eph. 5:26) so that when we stand before Your throne, my spouse will be more holy and godly because of my love.

Lord, grant us unity in the direction and decisions of our daily lives. When conflicts and misunderstandings arise, enable us to forgive each other quickly and completely. Help my thoughts, my tone of voice, my speech, and my actions be godly even in the most challenging of times (Note: 1 Pet. 3:9-15). Specifically, I pray to You, Lord, about __(name two areas in your marriage in which forgiveness is needed)__. Please forgive me for these, and give me the courage and humility to ask my spouse for forgiveness in these areas. Help me *"be kind to my spouse, tenderhearted, gracing my spouse with forgiveness the way that You have forgiven me"* (Eph. 4:32, personalized). Teach me to overlook the faults and weaknesses of __(spouse's name)__ because You have told us that *"love covers a multitude of sins"* (1 Pet. 4:8). Give me grace to see clearly what is happening in each challenging situation so I can embrace Your desires for reconciliation, truth, peace with grace, love, and a sense of humor—especially as we deal with the hard issues of life.

I realize I do not have the strength, resources, wisdom, or willpower on my own to be a good spouse without Your help, guidance, and power. Give me sensitivity to my spouse's needs. Help me to look for and support my spouse's strengths and qualities. Help me to be an encourager when my spouse needs encouragement and not be condemning when my spouse is doing wrong. Strengthen my ability to pray for and with my spouse, and to allow You to bring adjustment to his (or her) life. Help me to plan times when just the two of us will be together. I ask You to help me be a godly companion, a loyal friend, a satisfying lover, an unswerving supporter, and a _(fill in the blank with a desire you have for your marriage)._

I ask Your blessing on my spouse and on all that takes place in our master bedroom, Lord. In Jesus' name, amen.

Protection for Our Marriage

Lord, protect my marriage from anything that would damage, erode, or destroy it. Take out of our lives anyone who would come between us and tempt us. Help me immediately recognize and resist temptation when it presents itself. Caution my heart in places where temptation can flourish (Note: Matt. 6:13). I pray that any relationship either of us has or has had in the past will not derail any of Your purposes for our lives, as a couple and as parents. I also pray you will keep us from developing harmful relationships in the future.

Show me all the harmful ties we need to sever from our lives, whether they are people, agreements, entertainment or ideology. Show me where to set wholesome boundaries that line up with Your Word because You say, *"Guard your heart with all diligence, because out of it are the issues of life"* (Prov. 4:23).

Grant me the grace to face and deal with problems that rise in me; to never consider abandoning our relationship if it develops a nonworking part. Help us not to bring past relationship, hurts, controlling habits, or unloving communication to the forefront in ways that are harmful to each other or to our family.

I want to keep You at the center of my marriage and not expect from my spouse what only You can give—peace of mind, security, worth, and a true purpose for living. Where either of us has unrealistic expectations of the other, open our eyes to see them. May I never waver in my commitment and devotion to You and to my spouse, so that our marriage will be a source of joy.

Breaking Ungodly Soul Ties

In the name of Jesus and under His authority, I break, cancel, and demolish any ungodly soul ties that have been made through marital or pre-marital unfaithfulness. I claim the blood of Jesus to stand between me and _(name of person you are breaking the soul tie with)_ and invalidate the fleshly alliance this sin produced. I sever the emotional and sensual attraction that is attached to _(name of person)_ and I forgive myself for falling into this deception, self-indulgence, and unfaithfulness. I declare the blood of Jesus to be a permanent wall of separation between me and _(name)_. Heal our soul wounds from this sin with your dunamis resurrection power and the light of the presence of Jesus. In Jesus' name, amen. (If a spouse has been unfaithful, proclaim their names and if they will, ask them to pray this prayer in agreement with you.)

Lord, thank You for drawing _(name of spouse)_ and me to each other. Thank You for making us one in heart, soul, vision, and emotion; and for making us one physically. You have given us the treasure of one another in our marriage, and Your desire is that we drink deeply of marital love together. We desire to honor You through our total oneness—mind, emotions, will, and body. Thank You for the wonder and mystery of sex, for creating the two to become one flesh (Note: 1 Cor. 6:12-18). We pray for purity of heart, thought, and emotions as we love one another before You, because You say, *"let the marriage bed be undefiled"* (Heb. 13:5).

If one of us was unfaithful to You before we were married, forgive us and cleanse us as You have promised. If either one of us has been unfaithful during our marriage—physically or emotionally—forgive and cleanse us so that we can be whole and healthy again.

Preemptive Prayer for Protection from or Resolution of Abuse

Lord, protect our marriage from physical, emotional, or mental abuse. If there is any abuse, I pray it will be stopped immediately, dealt with firmly, and will not be repeated or become a highly destructive cycle in our family. I pray for the right counsel to address the severity of this situation quickly and for protection and covering for the one(s) suffering abuse. I pray for a godly counselor who can and will uncover underlying problems, past generational patterns, anger, and shame leading to any abusive behavior. I ask for zero tolerance on this issue, knowing that You do not intend for anyone to be physically or verbally abused. If a separation is required, I pray for two or three trusted prayer partners to join me in prayer regarding this decision. If there is an unhealthy co-dependent relationship, I ask you to change my heart to see the underlying root of rejection, abandonment or conditional love. If there is criticism, a mocking spirit, devisiveness, manipulation, or control issues, I ask those be brought to the light and that everything hidden will be revealed. Only then, can healing begin and healthy boundaries established.

For wounds or trauma suffered in the past, I ask for healing by You, our Great Physician, Protector, and Healer of this heart issue. For challenges we might face in the future, I pray for godly love to prevail, for exposure of intent and prevention before the fact—for healing without abuse. Thank You for Your promise, *"I will give you a new heart and put a new spirit in you; I will remove from you your heart of stone and give you a heart of flesh"* (Ezek. 36:26). Work on our hearts, Lord. In Jesus' name, amen.

Prayer for an Unsaved or Straying Spouse

Thank You, Lord, for ___(spouse's name)___. Please protect ___(spouse's name)___ from any confusion, deception, apathy, anger, bitterness, or temptation to violate our marriage covenant or refusal to embrace a love relationship with You. Shield ___(spouse's name)___ from the lies of the enemy (Note: Jn. 8:44), and guard ___(spouse's name)___ from being tormented by any impure, evil, negative, or damaging thoughts or actions. Protect our marriage as the precious, fragile, and amazing gift from You that it is.

I pray You will bring ___(spouse's name)___ into a right relationship with You, O God, through Jesus Christ (Note: Jn. 14:6). Your Word tells me You are a God who wants all men to be saved and to come to a knowledge of the truth (Note: 1 Tim. 2:4). Guide ___(spouse's name)___ to You so he (she) will desire a vibrant love relationship with You, Living God (Note: Matt. 22:37-39). Many voices have led ___(spouse's name)___ away from You, so I pray that You will help ___(spouse's name)___ hear Your voice above all others.

Lord, Your Word tells me, *"I have given you authority to trample on snakes and scorpions and to overcome all the power of the enemy;*

nothing will harm you" (Lk. 10:19). By the authority and power You have given me as a believer in Jesus Christ, I command any lying, deceiving, or destructive spirits to get away from __(spouse's name)__ . The enemy cannot have my spouse or destroy my marriage or family! I proclaim as true in You, Lord Jesus, that __(spouse's name)__ has a sound mind, a healthy marriage with me, and a close relationship with You (Note: 2 Tim. 1:7). By faith, I ask You to make it true in my marriage, my home, and in my family. I ask You to fill us completely with the Holy Spirit. Renew our respect for each other, our love, and our commitment we made before You when we made our marriage vows. In Jesus' name, amen

- **Note:** *The prayer for an unbelieving or straying spouse does not guarantee everything will be wonderful or immediately adjust in your marriage. Receptivity and obedience to the Word of God must be a part of both spouses' lives. If you are in an abusive marriage or a marriage in which an unbelieving or straying spouse no longer wishes to be married, please read 1 Corinthians 7 and talk with a godly pastor right away. Marriage, divorce, and singleness are all addressed in God's Word, so you must prayerfully consider each passage that applies in your situation in order to discern God's will for you. Please be sure you are listening to only God's voice and doing what He tells you in agreement with His Word.*

For Unmarried, Divorced, or Widowed Women

Lord, make this master bedroom the place where You initiate the most intimate relationship, where I can pour out my heart like water and be cleansed and restored—body, soul, and spirit. Let it be a sanctuary where I can listen and speak through prayer and find satisfaction. Let this room be the place where I can fall to my knees, cry from the depths of my heart in joy, pain, or worship, and express my deepest needs. When I become disappointed with the suffering in this fallen world, let this be the place where I can let the pain drive me toward You. You are my God who adores me and heals me. You promise to be my husband so I am confident you will protect and provide for me.

Lord, let this room also be a place where pivotal, heart-to-heart communication happens with my children, from listening to their needs to guiding them through difficult decisions. But more so, let my master bedroom be the place where I clearly hear that You love me, my Heavenly Father, and where healing comes for me, a daughter of the King. May Your voice speak more powerfully than other voices in my life and cause me to discover who I really am, to fall more deeply in love with the Father who delights in me, as you say, *"He will take great delight in you, He will quiet you with his love, He will rejoice over you with singing"* (Zeph. 3:17).

When I need privacy and a place to meditate, let the master bedroom be just that. King David wrote, *"On my bed I remember you: I think of you through the watches of the night"* (Ps. 63:6). Make this a place where I can replace my worries with meditation and thanksgiving.

Lord, make my master bedroom a place of intimacy, where vision is conceived and embraced. Give me a vision of total healing in my life and my children's lives—a vision of a life free of fear and worry, where I fall asleep listening to comforting verses and wake up refreshed. Give me a vision of restoration in my entire being: *"May God Himself, the God of peace, sanctify you through and through... The one who calls you is faithful and He will do it"* (1 Thess. 5:23).

Cause this room to also be a place of obedience and resolve. I know that as a Christian single, I cannot have sex outside of marriage, so help ME continuously determine to wait. *"God wants you to be holy and stay away from sexual sins. He wants each of you to learn to control your own body in a way that is holy and honorable. Don't use your body for sexual sin like the people who do not know God"* (1 Thess. 4:3-5).

Since you have said, *"Blessed are those who mourn, for they will be comforted"* (Matt. 5:4), let my heartache regarding those things I have lost find its end in this room, while You do Your work in me as I grieve, for you will turn my mourning into dancing (Note: Ps. 30:11). *"The Lord upholds all those who fall and lifts up all who are bowed down"* (Ps. 145:14). Help me to see my situation the way you do because you are protecting me from situations and people that are harmful. You are for me!

Lord, let this room be the place where I can fully trust Your leadership. You have the wisdom and understanding to guide me throughout the day. All resources belong to you. I trust You as my Protector, Leader, Husband, and Provider.

I thank You in advance for providing me with good companionship and loyal friends who can lift me up in trying times and whom I, in turn, can support. Thank You for giving me a community of believers to cut through the loneliness and isolation I often feel. I also pray that You will continue to provide me with theologically grounded prayer partners who will walk through this life by my side. You always provide

God-ordained prayer partners, so I thank you in advance for identifying them for me. In Jesus' name, amen.

ADDITIONAL SCRIPTURES

- *"For your Creator will be your husband; the Lord of Heaven's Armies is his name! He is your Redeemer, the Holy One of Israel, the God of all the earth"* (Is. 54:5 NLT).

- *"The Lord God said, 'It is not good for the man to be alone. I will make a helper suitable for him' … So the Lord God caused the man to fall into a deep sleep; and while he was sleeping, He took one of the man's ribs and then closed up the place with flesh. Then the Lord God made a woman from the rib He had taken out of the man, and He brought her to the man. The man said, 'This is now bone of my bones and flesh of my flesh; she shall be called "woman," for she was taken out of man.' That is why a man leaves his father and mother and is united to his wife, and they become one flesh"* (Gen. 2:18, 21-23).

- *"A wife of noble character is her husband's crown"* (Prov. 12:4).

- *"A wife of noble character who can find? She is worth far more than rubies"* (Prov. 31:10).

- *"Husbands, love your wives, just as Christ loved the church and gave himself up for her"* (Eph. 5:25).

- *"The husband should fulfill his marital duty to his wife, and likewise the wife to her husband. The wife does not have authority over her own body but yields it to her husband. In the same way, the husband does not have authority over his own body but yields it to his wife"* (1 Cor. 7:3-4).

CHILDREN'S ROOMS

As your children grow from the time they are born until they leave your home, their rooms may be the most important rooms in your home. Here is where they sleep and dream, where they awaken each day to face an increasingly difficult world. It is where they play, where they often "hang out" with friends, and where they go to hide from emotional pain, unkind words, and frightening incidents.

Praying God's blessing on your home and family should be high on your priority list. Your children (or grandchildren) need God's protection and guidance as they mature and become the exceptional individuals God created them to be. The importance of your prayers on their behalf cannot be underestimated. This grows even more evident when life circumstances try to knock them down.

Perhaps, like me, you've experienced an uncomfortable divorce. Divorce is difficult and painful. But there is life after divorce. With much prayer, a determined study of Scripture, and receiving godly counsel and guidance, I walked through it. God showed me it was necessary for the good of my children, as well as for my own good.

> CHILDREN NEED GOD'S PROTECTION AND GUIDANCE AS THEY MATURE AND BECOME ADULTS.

Now our kids have two destinations they call home—my home and their father's home. That being the case, it is extremely important for me to invite the Lord's presence into every room in my house. This is of even greater importance in the rooms where my children spend much of their time. I want them to feel my love and the love of the Lord from the moment they come into the house until the moment they leave. Like you, I want my children to enjoy healthy lives and experience the way the Lord replaces things that have caused them pain and restores the areas that are wounded and broken.

This same trauma and woundedness is experienced if you've lost a spouse, child, or loved one. The remaining family members suffer due to the pain and void in their lives. Faith in God is tested, abandonment issues arise and unconditional love is questioned. "This is when it is of the utmost importance to lean in and lean on God through prayer for comfort and guidance."

Here are just a few of the many verses I pray over my children and you can pray over yours as you ask for God's richest blessings to be on your families and homes.

- *"And pray in the Spirit on all occasions with all kinds of prayers and requests. With this in mind, be alert and always keep on praying for all the saints"* (Eph. 6:18).

- *"Pray continually"* (1 Thess. 5:17).

- *"Devote yourselves to prayer, being watchful and thankful"* (Col. 4:2).

Ask God for a spirit of wisdom and revelation every day with and for your children (Note: Eph. 1:17). You will find that if you *"watch and pray"* (Note: Matt. 26:41) for your children every day, God will give you insight, wisdom, and discernment. You will discover how to pray for them through any challenges they face, no matter what stage of life they are in. In prayer, you can address the problems and issues your child is currently facing. Remember, while a battle may be lost in a day, you can lose a whole war if you stop praying for your child.

Even when you do not know what to pray, or how to pray effectively for your children, God does. He will help you in those times.

> *And the Holy Spirit helps us in our weakness. For example, we don't know what God wants us to pray for. But the Holy Spirit prays for us with groanings that cannot be expressed in words.*
> ROM. 8:26 NLT

It is easy to get discouraged and grow angry with God. Don't! It is almost second nature to be overly controlling with our children as we try to force an answer to prayer. Again, don't! Our part is to pray. God's part is to answer. He answers prayer according to His good will, not according to our demands. He has promised to cause all things—ALL THINGS—to work together for good to those who love Him (Note: Rom. 8:28).

My dear friend, watch and pray and never give up. We accomplish far more by asking the Holy Spirit to come into our bodies, minds, and spirits than we can by trusting our own wisdom or strength. Make a commitment to pray; then watch what the Lord does. God's plan is better than we could ask, imagine, or hope for (Note: Eph. 3:20). His thoughts are not our thoughts, and His ways are not our ways (Note: Isa. 55:8-9). Your prayers are powerful and effective, so the enemy will do everything he can to keep you from praying. Don't stop praying!

> WATCH, PRAY, AND NEVER GIVE UP.

I have organized the activity of praying through your children's rooms into age-appropriate sections. The first section contains prayers you can pray for a child at any age. The following prayers are presented according to the chronological development of children: before birth, for a young child (birth to five years), for elementary age children (six to twelve years), for middle school age children (twelve to fourteen years), for those challenging teenage years (thirteen to nineteen years), and finally for college age young adults. I am anticipating that you will keep coming back to this guidebook through the years. Use it as a template to pray for the specific concerns which arise at their ages or seasons of life.

For centuries, many Christian parents have prayed a unique or special verse over each of their children. Some have also sung special songs which have proved a blessing in later years. God may have given you a specific name for your child, or shown you a specific verse before your child was born. He may even give you a specific promise or verse to rehearse at various seasons in your child's growth. If you have never done so, ask the Holy Spirit to lead you now, to give you a Scriptural promise, a song, or an affirmation to speak over your child. Then, be sure to record it in your journal so you can refer to it over and over again.

Here are several sample verses you can claim for your child:

1. Jeremiah 29:11-13
2. Lamentations 3:23
3. Matthew 11:28-30
4. Psalm 19:14
5. Psalm 23

6. Romans 8:32

7. Romans 8:38-39

Each child's room is filled with varying objects and furniture. Consider praying over some of these objects found in the appendix.

Activity Calendar, Child's Bed, Child's Dresser, Child's Blinds/Window Coverings, Child's Closet, Child's Mirror, Child's Study Desk, Computers, Fans, Floors, Globe/Map, Lamps (Lights), Mirrors, Music/Musical Instruments, Pets, Sports Equipment/Memorabilia, Stereo/CD Player/iPod™, Television/DVD Player, and Toys. (See: Appendix.)

Prayers for a Child of Any Age

COVERING WITH THE BLOOD OF JESUS

I declare the blood of Jesus to be all that is needed to cover the stain of sin on any and all of my children. I ask that Your blood, Jesus, be their covering and protection today in all that they do. It is by Your blood, Jesus, that we have right standing before You and Your throne, Lord. I proclaim the blood of Christ over each of my children today.

PRAYER FOR SAFETY AND PROTECTION

Lord, I speak out loud my prayer that You will help __(child's name)__ to be the best (he/she) can be. Thank You, Lord, You have not given us a spirit of fear, but of power and of love and of a sound mind (Note: 2 Tim. 1:7). Lord, I pray for safety and protection for my children from all harm and schemes of the enemy that seek to harm, destroy, or sidetrack their lives. I pray in agreement with Your Word that says, *"No weapon forged against you will prevail, and you will refute every tongue that accuses you"* (Isa. 54:17). Lord, I pray for __(child's name)__ to have a peaceful, calm spirit. I pray that when difficulties come, You will soothe (his/her) soul through Your presence, loyal wholesome friends, Your Word, and our family's support. Keep __(child's name)__ peaceful today because You are the Prince of Peace (See: Isa. 9:6). In Jesus' name, amen.

Lord, grant me a spirit of wisdom and revelation. I pray for insight and discernment as I seek to raise these children. You say, *"Train a child in the way he should go, and when he is old he will not turn from it"* (Prov. 22:6). I devote my children to You, our true Father. Teach me to hear and follow Your Holy Spirit as You stir my children's hearts, encouraging them and training them to live lives that are fully pleasing to You in every area (Note: Col. 1:9-14). Give me patience, strength, and wisdom to train, teach, discipline, and care for each child with their unique and special personality.

Lord Jesus, guide them as they make decisions regarding every aspect of their lives. Where there is any fear, anger, rebellion, manipulation, addictions, untruth, deception, anxiety, or any other area of disobedience, I ask for healing, release, and freedom from these challenges in Jesus' name (Note: Lk. 10:19).

I bring before You my concern about *(any area of concern that you have for your home or family)* . I ask for healing, release, and freedom from this area for *(child's name)* in the strong name of Jesus (Note: Jn. 8:32). I pray You will bring it to my mind to continue praying for this concern until it is conquered.

You have promised, *"From the Lord comes deliverance. May your blessing be on your people"* (Ps. 3:8). I pray for *(child's name)* to give (his/her) best to You. I pray *(child's name)* will love You with all (his/her) heart, soul, strength, mind, and body (Note: Matt. 22:37-39). I pray that impure thoughts or motivations to be "popular" at all costs will not be a driving force in *(child's name)* life. I pray (he/she) will resist the peer pressure of sex outside of marriage, drugs, abusing alcohol, bullying, addictions, pornography, or any "good" thing that takes too much time. I pray (he/she) will fill their minds with thoughts that are noble, right, pure, lovely, admirable, excellent, and praiseworthy before You (Note: Phil. 4:8) instead of the evil and selfishness the world offers. May __(child's name)__ experience the wonderful freedom of clear, positive, faith-filled thought processes to produce an excellent, God-honoring life (Note: 1 Cor. 10:31).

> **Note:** You should repeat the preceding portion of the prayer for each individual child.

Help me to understand each child's specific and ever-changing needs, and show me how to meet them. Give me discernment about what I allow into the home through TV, books, movies, video games, magazines, and computer activities because all of these influence our family. I ask You to shine Your light of truth and reveal anything or any area or action that is displeasing to You that will ultimately damage my children. You say, *"Guide me in Your truth and teach me, for You are God my Savior, and my hope is in You all day long"* (Ps. 25:5).

Give me a spirit of wisdom and revelation to know when to allow my children to venture out on their own to develop independence. I do not want to be overprotective, but neither do I want to allow my children to experience certain aspects of life too early. When they want to go into a store or to another child's home by themselves, show me the right timing and what to say in each situation. I am depending on You for moment-by-moment guidance when questions are asked and instruction is needed, guidance that will help shape their perception of the world. Shape their values so they will embrace their commitment to follow the wonderful plan You have for their lives. You promise a plan that is Your good, pleasing and perfect will (Note: Rom. 12:2). In Jesus' name, amen.

PRAYER FOR HEALTH AND BALANCE

Heavenly Father, I speak out loud and ask Your blessing because You love to give good gifts like health, balance, and freedom from sickness and disease. Your Word says, *"Dear friend, I pray that you may enjoy good health and that all may go well with you, even as your soul is getting along well"* (3 Jn. 2). Just as my child requires physical nourishment to grow and develop, I pray they will constantly find spiritual nourishment in You and Your Word because You remind us that *"man does not live on bread alone but on every word that comes from the mouth of the Lord"* (Deut. 8:3). Keep them safe from any accidents, disease, harm, or bad influences. In the name of Jesus, we break every hex, spell, curse, rebellion, vow or evil assignment.

Help me to raise my children to have a holy fear of You, leading them to be obedient in actions and respectful in thoughts, comments, and attitudes toward You, me, my spouse, and others (Note: Prov. 1:7). Let my children find fulfillment, contentment, and enjoyment in life while never losing sight of who You are and how important You are as their only true, dependable life coach. When they find fulfillment, help them to remember they are truly satisfied only when they're walking with You. When they feel contented, let them remember that You are their source of life and the giver of every gift in our lives. When they are filled with joy and happiness, help them remember that every happy event or feeling they have comes from You.

Give my children the fruit of Your Spirit: love, joy, peace, patience, kindness, goodness, faithfulness, gentleness, and self-control (Note: Gal. 5:22-23). Let these attributes be apparent in my children on a daily basis, as evidence of the Holy Spirit living inside them. Enable my children and me to live healthy, balanced, and peace-filled lives.

PRAYER FOR DEEPENING LOVE

Lord, establish close bonds of love between my children and me that will unite our hearts together.

"Make my joy complete by being like-minded, having the same love, being one in spirit and purpose" (Phil. 2:2). Show me how to communicate and express love to each of my children in ways they can understand; increase our desire to do what is best for each other with an ever-deepening, genuine love that can be clearly recognized and grasped by my child.

Grant me a spirit of wisdom to convey I am for them, to help them know I love them and am irrevocably committed to their best. Help me to be able to demonstrate my unwavering love to them in ways they can perceive, during good times, difficult times, and transitional times in their lives. Remind me to look into each of my children's eyes and tell them, *"I am so glad the Lord gave you to me as my child. I am so proud of you. I love you so much!"* Make me sensitive to unique times and opportunities to communicate love in special ways, too. Let them know I value their opinions and that I truly love them. In Jesus' name, amen.

PRAYER FOR PROTECTION FROM NEGATIVE INFLUENCES AND AN INVITATION FOR POSITIVE INFLUENCERS

Father God, Guardian of all that is good in our lives, I speak out loud my prayer asking You to protect my family, my marriage, and my children from anything that would influence us in negative ways or that would seek to destroy us. When someone tries to manipulate my children through lies or fear; when someone approaches children to experiment with drugs, alcohol abuse, sex, or rebellion against me, protect their hearts and lives. You have made me and my spouse their God-given authorities, so Lord I pray that no other relationship any of us has or has had in the past will steal from or adversely affect any positive progress we currently have in our relationship. I ask you to draw their friends to Yourself so they too become followers of God, and I ask you tor dissolve all ungodly connections in their lives.

Help me always to live in hope, not doubt or fear. Even when I face hectic times as a parent, I pray Your promise: *"to bestow on them a crown of beauty instead of ashes, the oil of gladness instead of mourning, and a garment of praise instead of a spirit of despair. They will be called oaks of righteousness, a planting of the Lord for the display of his splendor"* (Isa. 61:3). I pray that each of my children will develop strength of character (Note: Gal. 5:22-23), a fervent love for You and others (Note: Matt. 22:37-39), and the kind of life that invites Your blessing (Note: Col. 1:9-14). I pray we will turn to You, our Architect, our Hope, and our Lord, to secure our relationship and adjust every aspect of our lives to operate the way You intended.

All-knowing Lord, as I walk through my child's room now, I'm reminded to pray specifically for various areas of __(child's name)__ life. I pray (his/her) thoughts in this room would naturally gravitate toward enjoying You, God, every day because You tell us, *"Set your minds on things above, not on earthly things"* (Col. 3:2). I pray __(child's name)__ will invite You into this private part of (his/her) life. I ask that You will protect __(child's name)__ from being upset or worried. Instead of worrying, remind (him/her) to pray because You have told us, *"Don't worry about anything; instead, pray about everything. Tell God what you need, and thank Him for all He has done"* (Phil. 4:6 NLT). Cause __(child's name)__ petitions and praises to shape (his/her) worries into prayers, letting You know (his/her) concerns.

I pray that if __(child's name)__ is doing something wrong or something in conflict with Your commandments or laws, (he/

she) would be caught quickly. May _(child's name)_ be so filled with Your thoughts that You will give (him/her) a revelation of Your will for (him/her) and the wisdom to walk that out. Lord, I ask out loud right now for Your anointing for _(child's name)_ in providing (him/her) with good influencers and protection from bad influences. May Your richest blessings rest on _(child's name)_ and on this room, and thank You for the blessings You will bestow upon us. In Jesus' name, amen.

PRAYER FOR KIND SPEECH

Lord, I thank You for the gift of communication. I pray You will help my children be firm in their stand for God while guarding their tongue so the words they speak will build people up and not tear them down (Note: Eph. 4:29). Let their speech bring life and not destruction (Note: Prov. 18:20-21). You say, *"Life and death are in the power of the tongue, and those who use it must eat its fruit"* (Prov. 18:21).

Teach my children and me to put others first, to seek one another's well-being as a priority, as You have commanded in Your Word: *"Nobody should seek his own good, but the good of others"* (1 Cor. 10:24). We want to keep You at the center of our family, extended family, and friends, so that we do not expect from each other what only You can give us—true satisfaction, lasting security, perfect love, and a sense of our eternal worth in Your eyes.

Where any family member or friend have unrealistic expectations of others or is seeking for another member of the family to fulfill what You alone can provide, open their eyes to see it. Set them free. Teach my children to distinguish the essentials in life from the unimportant. May they cherish their relationship with You. Help them to desire a close relationship with the rest of the family and close relationships with faith-filled friends. Help them see that hurtful comments, fears of how they're perceived by others, or doubts in their abilities are not from You. They are simply lies that come from the father of lies, intended to deceive and destroy. Help them to recognize the answers You give through Your Word and through others because You love to answer prayers. In Jesus' name, amen.

Prayer Before Birth or for a Pre-School Child

Dear Lord, You gave (are giving) _(child's name)_ life and are loaning (him/her) to me. You made (are making) all the delicate, inner parts of (his/her) body and knitting (him/her) together in (my/my wife's) womb (Note: Ps. 139:13).

(Child's name) is exactly the way You desired: made in Your image, and, as You said, so wonderfully complex! Your workmanship is marvelous—and how well I know it (Ps. 139:14).

Help _(child's name)_ always to love You and reflect Your values, Your desires, and Your vision for the world because You have said that You want (him/her) to *"put on the new self, which is being renewed in knowledge in the image of its Creator"* (Col. 3:10). Grant (him/her) wisdom as (he/she) grows to discover the talents, gifts, and abilities You have given (him/her). Let (his/her) character fully develop at the right time to reflect You. I ask, when (he/she) makes decisions even as a child, (he/she) will demonstrate a heart for You, such as deciding to play nicely with children, not act selfishly, and not disrespecting (his/her) parents and authorities by (his/her) actions and attitudes. Your word says, *"Even a child is known by his actions, by whether his conduct is pure and right"* (Prov. 20:11).

Lord, You remind us that our children were in Your plan before You even made the universe: *"You saw me before I was born. Every day of my life was recorded in your book. Every moment was laid out before a single day had passed"* (Ps.139:16 NLT). Thank You, Lord, that every single day, every single week, month, and year are determined by You and Your plan for __(child's name)__ life. May Your blessing be on __(child's name)__ all (his/her) days. In Jesus' name, amen.

You should pray this prayer for each individual child.

Prayer for a Child in Elementary School

> **Note:** Before you begin praying, you may want to write Ephesians 1:17, *"I keep asking that the God of our Lord Jesus Christ, the glorious Father, may give you the Spirit of wisdom and revelation, so that you may know Him better,"* on a 3x5 card. Place the card in your child's room as a constant prayer request, then thank the Lord for each small step taken in that direction. The Lord answers prayers in a manner best for our children and us. It may not be what we asked for; it will be so much better. Pray specifically and in faith believing because God answers specific prayers specifically and general prayers generally.

Dear Lord, I ask Your blessing as I look around __(child's name)__ room and see all the things that indicate youth. As __(child's name)__ grows older, (he/she) will grow in height and weight but most importantly in stature. As it was said of Jesus, may it also be said of __(child's name)__: *"So Jesus grew both in height and in wisdom, and He was loved by God and by all who knew Him"* (Luke 2:52 NLT). Help __(child's name)__ grow physically, spiritually, mentally, emotionally, and socially in step with Your plan for (his/her) life, oh God.

I pray __(child's name)__ will distinguish (himself/herself) at an early age as one who seeks You with all (his/her) heart. Thank You for Your promise: *"In his heart a man plans his course, but the Lord determines his steps"* (Prov. 16:9). As __(child's name)__ grows and makes decisions, direct us in finding God-ordained friends, activities, teachers, school, neighborhood, church home, and relatives with whom to spend time. Give me a spirit of wisdom and revelation in knowing what to do at the right time to shape __(child's name)__ according to Your perfect plan.

Let __(child's name)__ be tender toward the wisdom You give in Proverbs 1-9, advice that will help (him/her) mature into fine, moral, and stable adults. Help (him/her) think through issues with wisdom, knowing how to respond in every situation with grace, truth, and skill. May __(child's name)__ always respect and fear You, and may Your wisdom be revealed to (him/her) through Your Word, the Bible, to direct (his/her) paths.

PRAYER FOR SON

May __(son's name)__ have the same blessings You bestowed upon David, as well as the same courage and heart (1 Sam. 17). David constantly sought You regardless of his circumstances. He was a key leader. He always took correction and responded quickly to it (Note: Ps. 51; Ps. 32). You have said of David, *"I have found David son of Jesse, a man after my own heart; he will do everything I want him to do"* (Acts 13:22). Make __(child's name)__ a man after Your own heart and a leader of Your people. Like David marching up to Goliath, may he demonstrate a willingness to take on giants in his life (Note: 1 Sam. 17). May he be a loyal friend to others (Note: 1 Sam. 18:1-4), show kindness to those less fortunate (Note: 2 Sam. 9), and use wise strategies in navigating through challenges (Note: 2 Sam. 7). Cause __(child's name)__ to see all of life through Your lens, God, and Your Word as David did (Note: Ps. 3). May my son reflect You, Your truth, and Your Spirit in his life by his attitudes and actions, just as David did (Note: Ps. 101).

PRAYER FOR DAUGHTER

May __(daughter's name)__ have the same characteristics as the noble woman described in Proverbs 31:10-31: trustworthy, dependable, intelligent, resourceful, loving, hardworking, compassionate to the poor and needy, and enriching to the lives of her family (vs. 10-11). May my daughter look for ways to do good things for others beginning with her family and then others in her sphere of influence (v. 11). Let her be a smart and hard worker, getting up early and planning her days well so she can maximize her time and resources most profitably (Note: Prov. 31:12-15). As she grows older, I pray __(child's name)__ will be intelligent and entrepreneurial in her investing and re-investing in people, time, and finances (vs. 16-19). I pray that __(child's name)__ will be an energetic, strong, hard worker (vv. 20-21). Lord, give her a heart for the poor and needy (v. 20). I pray she will carefully watch over her household so she can provide for it at the right time, and for the right time of year (vs. 22-25). I pray __(child's name)__ will have words that are wise and instructive to those around her (v. 26), words that flow from a loving heart, Lord (Note: Matt. 12:32-36). I pray her children and husband will respect and bless her by living according to the Bible, and honoring her because of the virtues she has modeled during her life (vs. 28-31).

> **Note**: You may want to take some time to read Proverbs 31:10-31 out loud in your daughter's room as a blessing for her. You can read Proverbs 3 out loud in your son's or

daughter's room. Insert their names at the beginning of each Scripture. God will use the spoken Word in your daughter's or son's room for good, both now and in the future.

PRAYER FOR SONS AND DAUGHTERS

Lord help me be able to express the value of Your Word to my children by the way I live. Help me be consistent with Your Word—in living, speaking, and through my actions—on a personal level. Let my example help them understand how to read Your Scripture and interpret it for today's life lessons. God, our Great Teacher, please instill in my children a love for Your Word so that they may grow in the grace and knowledge of our Lord and Savior Jesus Christ. *"To him be glory both now and forever! Amen"* (2 Pet. 3:18).

I ask out loud now for Your blessing on my children that they will grow up captivated by Your grace and desiring a close relationship with You. I thank You for the blessings You continue to shower on us. In Jesus' name, amen.

PRAYERS FOR A TEENAGE CHILD

Lord, I bring my teenager __(teen's name)__ before You now. I need Your help in encouraging (him/her) to become more independent, while becoming ever more dependent on You. My tendency is to hold on to (him/her), to try to prevent what I know will bring pain into (his/her) life. Yet to do so will keep (him/her) from being able to know You can redeem the mistakes (he/she) makes.

Holy Spirit, please produce the fruit of self-control in __(teen's name)__. May (he/she) stay within the boundaries I set in all areas, and may (he/she) do so without anger or frustration.

PRAYER FOR WISDOM WHEN TEMPTED

When my teen-aged children find themselves in potentially compromising situations (drugs, alcohol, sex outside of marriage, etc.), I pray they exercise self-control and think clearly in those situations just as Daniel did (Note: Dan. 1) or Mary did (Note: Matt. 1). Your Word says, *"No temptation has seized you except what is common to man. And God is faithful; He will not let you be tempted beyond what you can bear. But when you are tempted, He will also provide a way out so that you can stand up under it"* (1 Cor. 10:13). Protect them from potentially compromising situations, but help my teen(s) to see and take the way of escape You provide.

There are so many concerning aspects of life these days, Lord. At times, my tendency is to hold onto my teenager(s) all the more closely. What we see on TV, what we watch at the movie theater, what we read and listen to, and what is available to us on the internet, have tremendous influence on my teenager(s) thinking and desires. At times I want to block all media from our home, but I know You don't want us to hide from this world. I pray all I have taught my teenager(s) about You and Your values of morality will not be forgotten. When they encounter anything in this world that would seek to distract them from You, rise up as a shield for them. Give my teenager(s) the wisdom to walk with You through this world. Give them boldness to stand up to peer pressure. Instead of being influenced by evil, let them be an influence for good.

Heavenly Father, so much of today's media is filled with oppressive, violent, and promiscuous content. These feed powerful and harmful information into my teenager(s) subconscious mind and heart. Lord, I pray for Your protection for them from any harmful influences media imposes. Help them stand up to social pressure. Give them godly power over negative, ungodly words that pass through their thoughts and emotions.

PRAYER FOR RESPONSIBLE USE OF MEDIA

Lord, I pray my teenager(s) will be discerning of what is truly appropriate to listen to or watch. I pray they will only choose media that projects positive, constructive messages. May my teenager(s) reflect Your values through what they hear or see: *"Finally, brothers, whatever is true, whatever is noble, whatever is right, whatever is pure, whatever is lovely, whatever is admirable—if anything is excellent or praiseworthy—think about such things"* (Phil. 4:8).

I pray my teenager(s) will not be fooled by the false, glamorous marketing of the media. *"Don't be fooled by those who try to excuse these sins, for the terrible anger of God comes upon all those who disobey him"* (Eph. 5:6 NLT). Show my teenagers the natural consequences of bad decisions so they will see the results of a lifestyle that rejects You and Your values. Give them the strength and courage to stand firm in their beliefs and to be able to verbalize why certain media is not appropriate. Help them to have wide-open eyes to see when entertainers are not worthy of being emulated. You clearly state, Do not be misled: *"Bad company corrupts good character"* (1 Cor. 15:33). Grant my child a spirit of wisdom and revelation to see through the veneer to the real issues (Note: Eph. 1:17).

Lord, I lift my teen's speakers, headphones, and screens up to You and ask that every time they hear or view inappropriate media, they will feel a twinge of conviction. Convict them to understand this content and know it is not okay or conducive to their development. Holy Spirit, You have promised *"when he comes, he will convict the world of guilt in regard to sin and righteousness and judgment: in regard to sin, because men do not believe in me"* (Jn. 16:8-9). Please give my teenager(s) a hunger and thirst for righteousness.

> **Note:** *As you pray, you can might want to physically anoint your stereos, radios, speakers, computer, and iPods™ with oil, asking that they be used by the Lord to encourage your children.*

With my voice, I offer my prayer for my teenager(s) and their use of the computer. Along with the wonderful tool of the internet comes difficult challenges for them to face. They can be bombarded with pornographic information and advertisements, as well as approached by predators.

Father, as my children make choices about their online activities—social media connections, web searches, and email communications, I pray they will be wise and discerning, making choices that are healthy and positive rather than being drawn to harmful ones. Give them supernatural protection to avoid predators or imposters. Grant them the spirit of wisdom and discernment, and reveal the truth to my teenager(s) whenever they use the computer or other devices which connect to the internet.

Aloud, O Lord, I pray that when my teenager(s) chat with friends, they only express positive comments about other friends and refuse to indulge in gossip or negative, destructive conversations. Your Word says, *"don't use foul or abusive language. Let everything you say be good and helpful, so that your words will be an encouragement to those who hear them"* (Eph. 4:29 NLT). Make my teenager(s) a positive encouragement to others, which will draw others to them.

PRAYER FOR HEALTHY FRIENDSHIPS

I pray my teen(s) will choose to connect with other teens and young adults who will be good influences on them. Help them to disengage with those who are making poor choices regarding substance abuse, language, relationships with peers or adults, sexual behavior, and other inappropriate choices. Bring encouraging friends who desire to obey Your Ten Commandments and keep Your Word because they love You (Note: Jn. 14:21). Draw them to people who are positive in their speech (Note: Eph. 4:29), are honest in their communication (Note: Col. 3:9), are devoted to purity (Note: 1 Pet. 1:13-16), and are loyal friends (Note: Dan. 2:17-18). Make my teenager(s) this kind of friend to others as well. In Jesus' name, amen.

RELEASING YOUR COLLEGE/CAREER-AGE YOUNG ADULT

I speak out loud my thanks to You, Lord, for the precious gift of __(child's name)__, who is now old enough to pursue higher education or an emerging career. I recognize (he/she) was on loan to us, a gift for us to mold and shape in Your image. Thank You for the time we've had and the way our relationship has progressed and developed into what it is today. Even though __(child's name)__ won't be around as much, I pray You'll give us many opportunities to stay in touch and to maintain closeness so our family relationship can continue to deepen throughout these transitional years.

If there are any unresolved conflicts in our relationship at this point, reveal them to me, or give __(child's name)__ the confidence to talk with me, so I can do whatever I need to do to make it right. You have told me, "... *Go and be reconciled to your brother; then come and offer your gift [at the altar]*" (Matt. 5:24). Give us a sweet spirit of reconciliation. If __(child's name)__ is angry, rebellious, disrespectful, or ungrateful, I pray You will change (his/her) heart to be gracious and forgiving, sweet in spirit, respectful of You and of me, and deeply thankful for all Your wonderful gifts (1 Thess. 5:16). Give us unity, understanding, and reconciliation (wherever it is needed).

I ask Your blessing as I purposefully and deliberately release __(child's name)__ into the next step in the adventure You have for (him/her). You made (him/her), You love (him/her) more than I do, and You know what's best for (him/her). Lord, show me places where I continue to hang on to __(child's name)__, and enable me to release (him/her) into Your care, love, protection, and guidance. You have promised, *"But the Lord is faithful, and He will strengthen and protect you from the evil one"* (2 Thess. 3:3). Lord, continue to be the Guard, Protector, Truth, Defender, Strength, and Guide for (his/her) life. I expectantly wait to see the person he/she will become.

Lord, I speak out loud my prayer for __(child's name)__ and ask that You completely surround and protect (him/her) from harm. I pray __(child's name)__ will keep the Christian faith during these challenging years of transition. Protect his/her spirit, body, mind, and emotions from any kind of evil or harm. Your Word says, *"May God himself, the God of peace, sanctify you through and through. May your whole spirit, soul and body be kept blameless at the coming of our Lord Jesus Christ. The one who calls you is faithful and He will do it"* (1 Thess. 5:23-24). Lord, I ask You to fulfill this promise in *(child's name)* life. Let (him/her) get involved in good, wholesome activities among the friends and acquaintances (he/she) makes. Give (him/her) godly teachers, mentors, employers, and friends. I ask that all their weekend activities be fun-filled, wholesome activities, enjoyed in moderation and with common sense.

I continue to pray the full armor of God be *(child's name)* daily garment. As (he/she) ventures into the world, remind (him/her) to wear a belt of truth, a breastplate of righteousness, shoes of peace, a shield of faith, a helmet of salvation, and to carry the sword of the Spirit— the Word of God in their heart, in their mouth, and by their side.

I ask specifically that *(child's name)* will find Your protection from accidents, disease, injury, or any other physical, mental, spiritual, or emotional abuse (he/she) may encounter with roommates, classmates, work activities, or around ___(name of city)___ . I pray (he/she) will find their refuge in the shadow of Your wings and seek You because You have promised protection. I ask out loud now for Your blessing and anointing on my young adult in developing a desire to know and please You in all of (his/her) life.

PRAYER FOR AN ADOPTED OR ABANDONED CHILD

Lord, I thank You so much for our adopted child. I feel so blessed to have ___(child's name)___ added to our family through the gift of adoption, just as You added me to Your family through Your own creative process of adoption (Note: Eph. 1:5). Just like You chose me, You chose my adopted child to become a part of my family, carefully arranging events so we might be together.

> **Note:** Most adopted children were initially given up for adoption to a family who could care for them in a healthier lifestyle, or sometimes abandoned by or removed from their biological parents.

Jesus, You know the pain of being abandoned by Your Father as You cried out on the cross, *"My God, My God, why have you forsaken me?"* (Matt. 27:46; Mark 15:34). Whether through circumstances, tragedy, or by choice the feeling in my child remains as a sense of being abandoned or rejected. Regardless of the circumstances surrounding the adoption. God knew this was going to happen when He knit you in your mother's womb. He chose you! He has a super cool plan for you!

Lord Jesus, when You went to the cross, You took every curse upon You so that we might live a life of freedom and blessing (Note: Gal. 3:13) That includes the injury of abandonment. So I pray against any feelings of abandonment or rejection that my child may have. Let (him/her) feel loved by me, by our family, and most of all by You and I ask You to heal (his/her) soul and heart.

Remind _(child's name)_ , Lord, that You adopted (him/her) into Your family, that (he/she) is no longer an orphan, either literally or spiritually, but (he/she) has a loving earthly parent in me and a supremely loving spiritual Father in You.

I thank You, Lord that You have unconditional love for me and for _(child's name)_ . Show (him/her) the love You have for (him/her) in a real, practical, meaningful way today. Teach me to love my child utilizing thier love language.

Bless _(child's name)_ and help (him/her) to use (his/her) story of adoption as a way of telling the world about You and Your

Spirit of adoption. Let that truth be (his/her) guiding light and firm foundation as (her/she) grows and matures. Thank You most of all for Your promise throughout the Bible that You will neither leave us nor forsake us (Note: Deut. 31:6-8, Josh. 1:5). In Jesus' name, amen.

If you have more than one adopted child, repeat this prayer over each one.

ADDITIONAL SCRIPTURES

- *"Children are a heritage from the Lord, offspring a reward from him. Like arrows in the hands of a warrior are children born in one's youth. Blessed is the man whose quiver is full of them"* (Ps. 127:3-5).

- *"I will pour water on the thirsty land, and streams on the dry ground; I will pour out my Spirit on your offspring, and my blessing on your descendants"* (Isa. 44:3).

- *"And you are heirs of the prophets and of the covenant God made with your fathers. He said to Abraham, 'Through your offspring all peoples on earth will be blessed'"* (Acts 3:25).

- *"Children, obey your parents in the Lord, for this is right. 'Honor your father and mother'—which is the first commandment with a promise—'so that it may go well with you and that you may enjoy long life on the earth.' Fathers, do not exasperate your children; instead, bring them up in the training and instruction of the Lord"* (Eph. 6:1-4).

Make a commitment to pray; then watch what the Lord does.

Chapter Seven

Utility Spaces

CLOSETS

You might not consider praying over your closets, but you should. Your closets and your dressers are the places where you protect and preserve the clothing you wear. People around you instinctively assess your personality and expertise based on how you present yourself, and your clothing is a huge part of their assessment. As you determine your attire for the day, whether you will be working around your home, preparing for work, or planning a day of recreation, you must first go into your closet and/or dressers to locate what you will wear. Will it be appropriate? Will it compliment your personality and your life of faith? Will it project an image of competence, reliability, and faithfulness to God? As you pray over your closets, ask God to instill a sense of His approval for your choices.

Closet Prayer

Here I stand, ready to clothe myself for the day. Lord, let my attire never disguise who I really am. May I never hide myself in clothing to create a false or misleading impression of myself. I surrender each item in my closet to You, Lord. I want to dress in a way that informs others that I am the person You have made me to be.

More than these clothes, Lord, I want to step into the day, covered with the armor You have provided for me (Note: Eph. 6:13-17). In Jesus' name, amen.

PUTTING ON THE ARMOR OF GOD

- I gird my middle parts with Truth—not as a concept or a philosophy but the Person of Truth Himself, Jesus (Note: Jn. 14:6).

- I put on the breastplate of the righteousness of the Son of God, made available for me by His death and resurrection.

- For shoes, I put on the Gospel of Peace, so that everywhere I go today others will know You as the Prince of Peace and know the great gift of forgiveness of sins.

- I will carry with me the shield of faith: faith in Your love, faith in Your promises, and in Your forgiveness of my sins. Thus I will be able to extinguish all of the lies and accusations that come at me like flaming arrows from the evil one.

- My head covering will be the helmet of salvation, protecting my mind from lies that would tell me I am not enough or that I need to be different to be loved by You. Your helmet, Lord, will keep my thoughts centered on You and Your love for me. Bind my mind to the mind of Christ.

- Finally, I'll carry with me the sword of the Spirit, which is Your Word, written on my heart (Note: Heb. 8:10). It is also the Bible I carry in my hand, transport in my automobile, or place upon my desk. May my speech be audibly forthright in relating Scripture and its intent in the situations I encounter today.

Thank You for this armor which allows me to step into this day, knowing I am protected and that I am ready to do battle alongside You. In Jesus' name, Amen.

At this point, refer to the list of prayers for household objects and begin to pray over the things you may find in this closet.

ADDITIONAL SCRIPTURES

- *"I delight greatly in the Lord; my soul rejoices in my God. For he has clothed me with garments of salvation and arrayed me in a robe of his righteousness, as a bridegroom adorns his head like a priest, and as a bride adorns herself with her jewels"* (Isa. 61:10).

- *"And why do you worry about clothes? See how the flowers of the field grow. They do not labor or spin. Yet I tell you that not even Solomon in all his splendor was dressed like one of these. If that is how God clothes the grass of the field, which is here today and tomorrow is thrown into the fire, will he not much more clothe you—you of little faith?"* (Matt. 6:28-30).

- *"My brothers and sisters, believers in our glorious Lord Jesus Christ must not show favoritism. Suppose a man comes into your meeting wearing a gold ring and fine clothes, and a poor man in filthy old clothes and say, "Here's a good seat for you,' but say to the poor man, 'You stand there' or 'Sit on the floor by my feet,' have you not discriminated among yourselves and become judges with evil thoughts?"* (Jas. 2:1-4).

- *"Your beauty should not come from outward adornment, such as elaborate hairstyles and the wearing of gold jewelry or fine clothes. Rather, it should be that of your inner self, the unfading beauty of a gentle and quiet spirit, which is of great worth in God's sight"* (1 Pet. 3:3-4).

- *"I also want the women to dress modestly, with decency and propriety, adorning themselves, not with elaborate hairstyles or gold or pearl or expensive clothes, but with good deeds, appropriate for women who profess to worship God"* (1 Tim. 2:9-10).

BATHROOMS

Personal hygiene is an important part of personal, physical health. How you feel is greatly affected by how well you care for your physical body as well as for your spirit and your soul. As you pray over the bathrooms in your home, ask the Lord to give you sensitivity to His presence, that as you cleanse and groom your physical body, you will also allow Him to cleanse and groom your soul and make your spirit new.

BATHROOM PRAYER

Good morning, Lord! Thank You for allowing me to live another day. I ask You to cleanse me, this bathroom, and these toiletries from anything or any activity that has taken place here which is dishonoring or displeasing to You. Bring to my memory anything I may have knowledge of or unknowingly participated in that was against Your wishes, Lord. I ask forgiveness on behalf of me and my ancestors. I repent and renounce any alliance with these unacceptable practices and I align myself only with You.

As I prepare to face another day, I ask You to show me what You would like me to do. I give this day to You. Show me what is important for me to do today. You know what is best for me, so help me use the time and opportunities You are giving me to their greatest effectiveness for my life, for your You and for Your glory (Note: Eph. 5:15-16).

PRAYER FOR PROTECTION

You tell me in Your Word, *"For my thoughts are not your thoughts, neither are your ways my ways, declares the Lord"* (Isa. 55:8). I pray that You will guide my thoughts and help me prioritize my schedule according to Your divine plan. Give me the good sense to prioritize my day to complete the tasks, appointments, meetings, errands, phone calls, correspondence effectively, efficiently, and in a God-like manner.

I ask You for divine appointments, opportunities to meet with people You send my way. Help me to retain a godly persona, think godly thoughts, and speak with godly speech. Help me value my time, investing it with the right people for the right reasons. Protect me from listening to gossip and from gossiping about others. Give me patience when interruptions come so I don't overlook divine appointments You send my way.

As I prepare myself for the day, cleaning and moisturizing my skin, scrubbing blemishes and dirt from my body, and brushing my hair, please prepare my heart and mind by cleansing and purifying my thoughts. Lord, please forgive me of all my sins—intentional or unintentional. I claim Your purifying promise: *"But if we confess our sins to him, he is faithful and just to forgive us our sins and to cleanse us from all wickedness"* (1 Jn. 1:9 NLT).

Bring to my mind all of the things that are not pleasing to You. Cause me to feel any twinge of conviction in my spirit and heart which helps me realize what I need to confess and repent of, Father of Truth. Please help me to discipline my mind to think as Jesus would in each situation because I have the mind of Christ (Note: 1 Cor. 2:16). Help me live a life filled with love, following the example of Christ. He loved us and offered himself as a sacrifice for us, a pleasing aroma to God (Note: Eph. 5:2). I ask that my speech and actions will be gracious and truthful (Note: Lk. 4:22). Help me to speak the truth in love today, just as Jesus did (Note: Eph. 4:26-32).

As I put on deodorant, perfume or cologne, help me remember to be a fragrant aroma of Christ today, pleasing to You in every way. *"Let me spread the knowledge of Christ everywhere (I am found), like a sweet perfume. My life is a Christ-like fragrance rising up to God"* (2 Cor. 2:14-15 NLT, personalized).

Lord, equip and use me as a valiant warrior in Your army today. *"I do not fight against flesh-and-blood enemies, but against evil rulers and authorities of the unseen world, against mighty powers in this dark world, and against evil spirits in the heavenly places"* (Eph. 6:12 NLT, personalized).

When I look in the mirror, may the reflection I see be a reflection of You, Lord Jesus. That is my goal—to be more like You (Note: Rom. 8:29-30). You created a beautiful child of God, and should I look in the mirror and wish my hair were longer, shorter, straighter or curlier; or my nose and eyes were formed differently, convict my heart to stop longing to look like someone else. I thank You, dear Lord, that I am Your child, just the way You made me. I look exactly the way You planned for me to look, Your beautiful daughter (Note: Ps. 139:14).

This I declare about the Lord: *"He alone is [our] refuge, [our] place of safety; He is [our] God, and [we] trust Him. For He will rescue [us] from every trap and protect [us] from deadly disease. He will cover [us] with his feathers. He will shelter [us] with His wings. His faithful promises are [our] armor and protection"* (Ps. 91:2-4 NLT, brackets added).

Today, as I go out into the world full of dangers and challenges, I don't know what I'll encounter. I can't possibly see or know what will happen to my loved ones or in the places where I will go. God, El Roi, the God Who Sees, You are the only One who knows what awaits me today. Oh Lord, my Protector, I pray Psalm 91 for my spouse, kids, family, and extended family, and _(insert name)._ I pray specifically for _(list individual names)._

I ask today, dear Lord, that as I brush my hair, remind me to put on the helmet of salvation. Lord, please help me wear the helmet so it can never be removed, to protect my mind to only think godly thoughts (Note: Eph. 6:17). Lord, I ask You to remove any areas of darkness or deception in my life. Please flood my body, my life, my room, and my house with Your light.

Lord, as I put on my shirt, remind me to put on the breastplate of righteousness (Note: Eph. 6:14). Lord Jesus, please place the body armor of God's righteousness in place so it cannot be removed and so it protects my heart. Please surround me with guardian angels to protect me wherever I go, and may a hedge of protection be placed around me. You have told me that if I make You my refuge, if I make the Most High my shelter, no evil will conquer me; no plague will come near my home. For You will order Your angels to protect me wherever I go. They will hold me up with their hands so I won't even hurt my foot on a stone (Note: Ps. 91:10-12).

Help me today to be protected by the shield of faith in Jesus Christ and Your wonderful Word, the Bible (Note: Eph. 6:16). I pray, Lord, that the belt of truth will fit well on us so it can't be removed. Please open our eyes and ears so we can see and hear Your Word (Note: Eph. 6:14).

Lord Jesus, I pray we will put on the armor of shoes You provide spiritually—so I am at peace with You and with others (Note: Eph. 6:15).

Lord, I trust and obey Your Word, which is also the sword of the Holy Spirit (Note: Eph. 6:17). Fill every cell and fiber in my body with Your Holy Spirit and with a vision of Your protection, guidance, and love through Your Word, because You have said, *"All Scripture is God-breathed and is useful for teaching, rebuking, correcting and training in righteousness, so that the man of God may be thoroughly equipped for every good work"* (2 Tim. 3:16-17).

Lord, I ask that You fill all of us with the fruit of the Holy Spirit: *"But the fruit of the Spirit is love, joy, peace, patience, kindness, goodness, faithfulness, gentleness and self-control. Against such things there is no law"* (Gal. 5:22-23).

Lord, I also want to pray daily to You the prayer of Jabez. I know lives are radically changed and enhanced by praying this prayer:

Jabez cried out to the God of Israel, *"Oh, that you would bless me and enlarge my territory! Let your hand be with me, and keep me from harm so that I will be free from pain"* (1 Chron. 4:10). Lord, we pray that You will bless us right here and right now. Open wide our territories to share Your name and love. For those in our family who do not have a relationship with You yet, I pray You will lead them to Your love. Protect us with Your hand, and shelter us from evil so it will not cause pain.

So I pray Your blessing on my bathroom today, Lord.

Now would be an ideal time to consult the list of prayers for the various objects you might find in your bathroom. I recommend you memorizing the Prayer of Jabez and recite the last line when confronted with a serious or unsettling situation. Here are a few of my suggestions: Books/Reading Material Candles, Chairs, Flowers, Glasses or Cups, Mirrors, Plants, Positive Words/Messages, Stereo/CD Player/iPod™, Vessels/Vases, Water. (See: Appendix.)

ADDITIONAL SCRIPTURES

- "The law of the Lord is perfect, refreshing the soul" (Ps. 19:7).

- "He makes me lie down in green pastures, He leads me beside quiet waters, He refreshes my soul" (Ps. 23:2-3).

- "When you, God, went out before your people, when you marched through the wilderness, the earth shook, the heavens poured down rain, before God, the One of Sinai, before God, the God of Israel. You gave abundant showers, O God; you refreshed your weary inheritance. Your people settled in it, and from your bounty, God, you provided for the poor" (Ps. 68:7-10).

- "The Lord makes firm the steps of the one who delights in him" (Ps. 37:23).

- "I will make them and the places surrounding my hill a blessing. I will send down showers in season; there will be showers of blessing" (Ezek. 34:26).

LAUNDRY ROOM

"Mom, where is that pink skirt I wore last week? I'm planning to wear it to school."

"It's with the other dirty clothes."

How many times have I given that answer? As my children were growing up, the laundry room was a revolving door. It probably is in your house as well. A mountain of laundry quickly piles up in a busy house. A mountain of dirty stuff tends to pile up in our lives, too, if we don't pay attention.

It is possible to have such a large amount of "dirty laundry" in our lives, we feel it would take far too long to deal with it. So, why bother?

Jesus specializes in cleaning our lives and removing the stains of sin, no matter how big, no matter how long they have been a part of our lives. He loves to forgive and cleanse. Whether it has been days, weeks, or months since you asked Him for forgiveness and cleansing, He has promised to hear and answer your prayers with His gracious love. Even if it has been years … He still is ready to forgive and cleanse your life.

> JESUS SPECIALIZES IN CLEANING OUR LIVES AND REMOVING THE STAINS OF SIN.

As you ask God to bless the laundry room of your home, pray especially for each family member and for the Lord to clean out the dirty stuff from each one's life. (You may interchange child, son, daughter, husband, wife, a loved one or yourself in this prayer.)

LAUNDRY ROOM PRAYER

Lord, I ask Your blessings upon the laundry room. As I am sorting and cleaning the clothes for my family, may I be just as careful to examine the soiled and stained spots in my life and my family's lives. I have to be able to see the spots before they can be removed. I cannot remove stains I cannot see, so I ask You, Lord, to expose my sins and shortcomings and show me what I am doing that needs to be brought before You for forgiveness.

Lord, as I clean and organize my children's clothing for the week, help me remember to pray for each child and their spiritual, emotional, mental, and physical needs. I pray You will encourage my children and cause them to grow into adulthood, holding onto and delighting in Christian values.

As I fold the shirts and blouses, I pray their hearts and bodies will be striving to stay free of the "wrinkles" of sin. I pray that as they wear their blouses and shirts, they will run, jump, and play in a healthy way. I ask that they will stand confidently and stand tall because they know they are Your special chosen children. The shirt covers their hearts, and so I pray that each child will have a soft heart that is responsive to You and Your truth through Your Word. Help them to be open to my direction as a loving parent. I pray this for my children: *"I will give you a new heart and put a new spirit in you; I will remove from you your heart of stone and give you a heart of flesh"* (Ezek. 36:26).

Lord, give us deeper wisdom, knowledge, and discipline in every area of our lives. I ask Your blessing on this laundry room and all the clothing that leaves this room, being worn by this family and by extended family members. I ask that You cleanse and purify us to do Your will. In Jesus' name, amen.

Don't forget to use the prayers for the individual objects you'll find in the laundry room. A few suggestions would include: Bed/Sheets/Pillows, Blankets, Colors, Doors, Floors, Lamps (Lights), Table, Work Desks. (See: Appendix.)

ADDITIONAL SCRIPTURES

- *"Have mercy on me, O God, according to your unfailing love; according to your great compassion blot out my transgressions. Wash away all my iniquity and cleanse me from my sin"* (Ps. 51:1-2).

- *"I will bring Judah and Israel back from captivity and will rebuild them as they were before. I will cleanse them from all the sin they have committed against Me and will forgive all their sins of rebellion against Me"* (Jer. 33:7-8).

- *"But if we confess our sins to Him, He is faithful and just to forgive us our sins and to cleanse us from all wickedness"* (1 Jn. 1:9 NLT).

THE BASEMENT/CRAWL SPACE

In many homes, basements become multi-purpose rooms, places to hang out, useful for storage, and the space where utilities are best accessed. In the Midwest, where I live, most homes have a basement. This is partially for protection against severe weather—tornadoes and severe storms. Amazingly, however, tornado sirens scream their warnings; most of my neighbors go outside to look for the tornado, rather than retreating to a protected space! Not a recommended course of action.

Basements sometimes become laundry rooms or extra bedrooms, garages or workshops. They also become dens, game rooms, and sometimes personal gyms. They may even be used for creative arts such as sewing or woodworking. And some are just empty areas where dust and mold collect.

Most basements could use a good cleaning. If we shined a bright light into the corners of our basements, we might just be surprised at what is living there. In the same way, we also need to expose our lives to the light of God's truth so that every hidden area is illuminated. You do this by asking God to reveal any hidden areas of darkness in your life. Then, sit quietly and listen for His voice to speak to your heart to tell you what is displeasing to Him and how to remedy it. Bad habits have a way of becoming invisible, hidden in the dark corners of our hearts. It could be that you have an unhealed wound in your soul which prompts you to repeat an unhealthy, ungodly habit. It could be something you never even imagined, but it's there, like a nagging ache.

> WE NEED TO EXPOSE OUR LIVES TO THE LIGHT OF GOD'S TRUTH.

Pray for the Holy Spirit to reveal hidden areas in the lives of family and friends who enter your basement. The Scriptures say: Have nothing to do with the fruitless deeds of darkness, but rather expose them. For it is shameful even to mention what the disobedient do in secret (Note: Eph. 5:11,12).

While you are shining a light in your basement, you might take a look at all the things you have stored down there. Are you a pack rat, one who rarely throws anything out? Perhaps it's time to go through those boxes and shelves and get rid of what you no longer use. You don't need it, it is merely clutter that takes up valuable space.

In the same way, you may need to search your heart. See if there are things you're holding on to that you really need to let go. Are you holding a grudge against someone who hurt you?

Forgive them and get rid of it. Are you hoarding anxieties and worries? Give them over to the One who cares for you (Note: 1 Pet. 5:7). You can use the space in your heart to fill with love, compassion, and the joy of the Lord.

BASEMENT PRAYER

Father, I ask Your blessing upon all who descend the stairs into this basement. May all who come down into the basement carrying worries, anxieties, guilt, or shame, sense Your peace and leave them at Your feet before they ascend the stairs again.

Let all conversations and activities in this space bring honor and glory to You. May everything done here be glorifying to You in all ways, Lord. Let no one think they can get away with things down here just because this space is out of sight from the rest of the house. Holy Spirit, be very present in this basement so that all will know God alone is the Lord of our home, no matter which room they are in.

Lord, I thank You for all the material blessings You have given us. I ask You to quicken my spirit so I may discover areas of excess I should be cleaning out, things I have stored, clutter that has accumulated, and items I no longer need or use. As I rid my home of them, may the items be helpful to other people as I give them away.

Thank You, Lord, that the earth is the Lord's, and everything in it, the world, and all who live in it (Note: Ps. 24:1). I commit everything—all that I am and have—to You, for Your use, Oh Lord. As I look at the items we have stored in our basement, I ask You, Lord, to help me see them through Your eyes, to contemplate how they could be used to help others.

Thank You for the exercise equipment we use. Help us to be faithful and consistent in its use as we strengthen our bodies and maintain our health. I pray for safety as we use it. I pray that my family and I will honor You with our bodies. When I am exercising and am tempted to quit, give me the renewed desire to see it through to the end, knowing that persevering to the completion of a workout will translate to perseverance in life.

Lord, You are the ultimate Artist. When we use this basement for art and craft projects, we ask that You inspire our vision.

Anoint our eyes, minds, and hands to make us productive to create unique and inspired art forms/pieces. You have gifted people throughout history with great creative skills to put to use for You (Note: Ex. 36:1-2).

Please give us the vision and creative capacity to produce the best artistic expressions of which we are capable. Lord, we know You appreciate and admire the wonders of art; they are pleasing to Your eyes. We behold Your creativity every day in the nature that surrounds us. We ask that You instill in us the desire and the talent to develop our God-given, artistic and creative gifts, because You remind us, Whatever you do, work at it with all your heart, as working for the Lord, not for men (Note: Col. 3:23).

Just as our art projects take time to complete, we, too, are a "work in progress." Thank You, Lord, that You have promised: *"Never will I leave you; never will I forsake you"* (Heb. 13:5). Just as we stick to a project to its completion, so You stick with us until Your Son, Jesus Christ, is formed in us fully (Note: Rom. 8:28-30). May we always remember Your promise, Lord, for we are God's workmanship (artwork), created in Christ Jesus to do good works, which God prepared in advance for us to do (Note: Eph. 2:10). Thank You that You have made us Your work in progress and Your masterpiece, Lord.

We ask out loud right now for Your richest blessings on every person who enters this basement to remember that he (she) is Your masterpiece, Your work in progress. In Jesus' name, amen.

Crawl Space Prayer

Lord, I thank you for this home and all that it means to our family. I pray your blessings over this crawl space that the underlying problems and the spiritual influences which would work against us would be removed. We want our home to be a place bringing glory to You in every way. In the same manner in which we prayed over and blessed the foundation of this home, let this crawl space be protected and stable. In Jesus' name, amen.

One final thing: when you pray over your basement, consult the list of prayers for individual household items. Some prayers you might consider focusing on would include: Art/Posters/Created Objects/Design & Crafting Tables, Chairs, Chess Set/Board Games, Doors, Food, Music/Musical Instruments, Sports Equipment, Memorabilia, Stairs/Steps, Television/DVD Player, Toys, and Work Desks. (See: Appendix.)

ADDITIONAL SCRIPTURES

- *"The Lord will send a blessing on your barns and on everything you put your hand to. The Lord your God will bless you in the land He is giving you"* (Deut. 28:8).

- *"Our barns will be filled with every kind of provision"* (Ps. 144:13).

- *"Do not store up for yourselves treasures on earth, where moths and vermin destroy, and where thieves break in and steal. But store up for yourselves treasures in heaven, where moths and vermin do not destroy, and where thieves do not break in and steal. For where your treasure is, there your heart will be also"* (Matt. 6:19-21).

THE GARAGE AND THE AUTOMOBILE(S)

Like the basement, a garage can easily become a place where clutter and unused items collect. Designed for the protection of automobiles, garages easily become little more than junk rooms.

In our contemporary world, we spend significant time traveling. Your automobile is an important part of your family's life, transporting you and your family to the places you need to go. It provides shelter as you travel, convenience to cover greater distances, and comfort during those journeys.

If your garage has become cluttered and filled with unnecessary, unusable items, return to the basement prayers and precepts and ask God to help you set it in order, substituting garage for basement in those prayers.

Garage and Automobile Prayer

Lord, I ask Your blessing on this utility space where our car(s) is/are parked and protected from the elements. I surrender this space to you and ask you to remind us of its importance to our family's well being.

Father, bless us each time we leave our home through this garage. Protect us whether we are driving or riding in this/these vehicle(s). Keep us safe on the roads we travel. Keep us alert to the actions of other drivers and to road conditions. Set a supernatural hedge of protection around us regardless of how far we drive.

Father, You say You will direct the way we should go: *"In all your ways acknowledge Him, And He will make your paths straight"* (Prov. 3:6 NASB). We pray You will guide our ways clearly. It is our desire to follow You and trust You always, so guide us by Your Holy Spirit. Let us travel through our lives with confidence knowing we are following You and we can trust Your grace to hold us close. Help us rely upon you each time we leave through these doors, whether we do so on foot, on bicycles, or in our vehicles.

Thank You, Lord, for our cars recognizing them as a blessing from You. We pray Your blessing on them and also ask You to keep our cars from mechanical failure. We know that You are the Ruler over all things, so we place these in Your hands for Your safekeeping. Father, don't let me get attached to physical things. Keep me from coveting new cars for status or pride. Thank You for the vehicles we have. Help me to be content in a world that tells me to continuously desire new things.

Lord, I also ask Your blessing on games we have here in the garage. We love to play games that bring us closer as a family. Bless our times as we play together. Let us be drawn together as we enjoy times together remembering to be kind and encouraging while playing these games. Lord, our laughter makes You happy. A cheerful heart is good medicine (Note: Prov. 17:22).

I ask Your blessing on the tools we keep in this garage. The garden tools—the rakes, shovels, and hoes. Thank You for the garden we can tend—let it remind us of Your law of sowing and reaping. Whatever we put in the ground, that is the type of fruit we will harvest—help us always to sow good seed in the world around us. Bless the mechanical tools—the hammers, the screwdrivers, the wrenches, etc. Thank You for the wisdom and skills necessary to use these tools. Keep everyone safe who uses these tools.

Bless the bikes, skateboards, scooters and outdoor gear. Protect those who use them. Let them sense Your pleasure as they play on these, as they are ways we can get out and enjoy the world You created. Let us be reminded of Your beauty, of Your majesty and power as we enjoy the outdoors.

Lord, bless us when we return through these doors. When we come back home, let us be sure to leave our cares and worries at Your feet. Help us to leave the world behind as we enter our sanctuary. Let us always know Your peace and presence in our home.

Before you pray, turn to the prayers for everyday objects (See: Appendix) and select some prayers you want to use while you're praying over your garage and everything in it. You might decide to choose such prayers as: Buildings/Structures, Cars, Keys, Lamps (Lights), Locks/Security/Protection, Music/Musical Instruments, Pets, Sports Equipment/Memorabilia, and Stereo/CD Player/iPod™.

ADDITIONAL SCRIPTURES

୬ *"Therefore my dear brothers and sisters, stand firm. Let nothing move you. Always give yourselves fully to the work of the Lord, because you know that your labor in the Lord is not in vain"* (1 Cor. 15:58).

- "Therefore, my dear friends, as you have always obeyed—not only in my presence, but now much more in my absence—continue to work out your salvation with fear and trembling, for it is God who works in you to will and to act in order to fulfill his good purpose" (Phil. 2:12-13).

- "That is why we labor and strive, because we have put our hope in the living God, who is the Savior of all people, and especially of those who believe" (1 Tim. 4:10).

HOME OFFICE

With the innovation of personal computers, more people are maintaining an office in their family home. Working from home presents challenges not apparent in a traditional workplace environment. Balancing time between family and work becomes difficult. Each requires a substantial amount of time, effort, and focus, and with a home office the boundaries are blurred. The great advantage to having an office in your home can also become the greatest disadvantage. It is simply that you are close to your spouse and children, sometimes too close, involving you in the ups and downs of their daily lives, sometimes unnecessarily.

If you value and enjoy your work, it can become a challenge to close the door to the home office and be with your family—especially at night and on weekends. A home office offers continuous access to e-mails, phone calls, and a never "leave the office at the office" mentality. The result is that the family suffers. We may be physically there, but we are not mentally there with them.

God's word instructs us as employees to be diligent, working honestly and sincerely for our employer, not just when they are watching, but throughout the required work schedule. *"Serve them [your employer] sincerely because of your reverent fear of the Lord. Work willingly at whatever you do, as though you were working for the Lord rather than for people"* (Col. 3:22-23 NLT, brackets added). Whether we work at a home office or in an office building, our desire is to please the Lord by working diligently, focused, and effectively for Him. But working in a home office often extends beyond reasonable working hours. This tension between work and family is why it is imperative we pray God's richest blessings, balance, and protection on this important area of our family homes. When you work in a home office environment, you need to be faithful to a work schedule that provides ample time for involvement with your family, your church, and your community.

HOME OFFICE PRAYER

Lord, I pray You will bless this home office and the work completed in this room. Help me prioritize my work so I will properly balance my family and work goals. I pray You will help me maintain a focused work ethic allowing me to adequately provide for my family, yet be flexible enough for God-ordained interruptions. Remind me Your Word says, *"Be very careful, then, how you live—not as unwise but as wise, making the most of every opportunity, because the days are evil"* (Eph. 5:15-16).

When my schedule become overburdened, help me prioritize my work and family commitments asking You what are the God-ordained priorities so I will not shortchange my family. I ask for godly wisdom, understanding, discernment, and knowledge for all situations.

I pray I will be able to earn a good living in my home office and have favor with others (Note: Lk. 2:52). I pray I will never become obsessed with money, the game, the power, the ego, or the pride that can come with professional success. Give me insight as to how much time I should spend on each task and show me which items are "A" priorities and "B" priorities. Teach me to work in a smarter way.

As I use the Internet, protect me from wasting time, becoming distracted, or pursuing ungodly fixations. I pray You will help me use the Internet tools to maximum my business yet not be overly dependent on it. You have given me work to do and for that I am thankful. Help me face each work project with enthusiasm.

Lord, I give You each moment of my workday. I commit my ways, my actions, my calendar to You—let all of my appointments be "God appointments." Send me wise and godly business associates, customers, and clients with whom I can do business. I pray the clients who are not godly will see the light within me and be drawn toward You, Lord. Your desire for me is to let my light shine before men, that they may see my good deeds and praise my Father in heaven (Note: Matt. 5:16).

Give me wisdom, sound judgment, and good planning in all of my work activities, meetings, and interactions. I pray that when I hit stumbling blocks along the way which initiate procrastination, You will help me become motivated and energetic to complete the work necessary. You remind me, *"Whoever works his land will have plenty to eat, but the one who chases unrealistic dreams has no sense"* (Prov. 12:11, GW).

Oh, Lord, many times I am going to be confronted with the temptation to cut corners. There will be times that telling a half truth will seem to be the most convenient course of action. Holy Spirit, I ask before I say or do anything that is illegal, immoral, or unethical, You will bring conviction to my heart. Do not let me bring shame to Your name by my actions. You have reminded me, *"Good planning and hard work lead to prosperity, but hasty shortcuts lead to poverty"* (Prov. 21:5 NLT).

May I always be exemplary in my words and deeds as a business person. When tempted to do wrong, prompt me to remember Your definition of success is not equivalent to the world's definition. I want to bring You glory in all I do and say, my Lord. May I have favor with those whom I encounter in my work, both personal and financial, receiving the just compensation I deserve for the work I do.

Father, I ask that You keep fear far from me—that I will not fear any person for what they can do to me. Help me remember You are always with me. I pray I will not fear financial loss for You are my Provider. We read, *"And my God will meet all your needs according to his glorious riches in Christ Jesus"* (Phil. 4:19). Gracious Lord, You have provided the career I have. I remember that You are my source and I am grateful for Your word reminds me, *"But remember the Lord your God, for it is He who gives you the ability to produce wealth"* (Deut. 8:18).

Father, in times of unemployment and underemployment, "the way things have always been" just might not be enough. Grant me creative ideas to be of great value to my employer (or, if you are self-employed, ideas to stay busy for those who hire your services). Should the time arise for me to seek a new job, I pray You would guide my search, giving me wisdom in the areas where I need to look. Encourage me through times of disappointment and provide me with a perfect and complementary fit, so that I might be employed in the place where You desire. When I encounter a wall show me a way around it. You are the Creator and all creative ideas flow from You. I thank You for all the ideas You give to me.

Lord, I ask Your richest blessings on this home office and ask You to give me balance, protection, and successful work. In Jesus' name, amen.

Some objects in your home office you may consider praying over could include: Activity Calendar, Clocks, Computers, Floors, Globe/Map, Lamps (Lights), Phones, Positive Words/Messages, Table, and Work Desks. (See: Appendix.)

ADDITIONAL SCRIPTURES

- *"By the seventh day God had finished the work He had been doing; so on the seventh day He rested from all His work. Then God blessed the seventh day and made it holy, because on it He rested from all the work of creating that He had done"* (Gen. 2:2-3).

- *"When He saw the crowds, He had compassion on them, because they were harassed and helpless, like sheep without a shepherd.*

Then He said to His disciples, 'The harvest is plentiful but the workers are few. Ask the Lord of the harvest, therefore, to send out workers into his harvest field'" (Matt. 9:36-38).

- *"For this reason, since the day we heard about you, we have not stopped praying for you. We continually ask God to fill you with the knowledge of his will through all the wisdom and understanding that the Spirit gives, so that you may live a life worthy of the Lord and please Him in every way: bearing fruit in every good work, growing in the knowledge of God"* (Col. 1:9-10).

Whether it has been days, weeks, or months since you asked Him for forgiveness ... He has promised to hear and answer your prayers with gracious love.

CHAPTER EIGHT

Property Maintenance

HOUSEKEEPING

Wouldn't it be nice if your house was self-cleaning? It would be, but that doesn't happen. You probably find yourself (if you're a mom) repeating that famous, anonymous quotation, "This house isn't going to clean itself!"

Unfortunately, it takes continuous effort to keep dirt, spills, and clutter from taking over. Every home needs daily cleaning. Every home needs regular deep-cleaning as well in order for the household to function as it should and life to be livable.

In the same way, homes need regular "holy housecleaning" to keep the family functioning the way the Lord intends. Sometimes this is as simple as spending time together in prayer for daily needs. Other times, however, require a "deep spiritual cleansing." These times include praying through the rooms of the home and around the property, playing music that exalts God, reading specific Scripture or playing an audio Bible recording in the rooms or places your family uses the most.

> IN TIMES OF GREAT STRESS IN YOUR HOME, YOU SHOULD SPEND MORE TIME IN SPIRITUAL "HOUSECLEANING."

In times of great stress in your home, you should spend more time in spiritual "housecleaning." If one of your children is in rebellion, you need to spend time in prayer in their room asking the Lord for discernment. Ask if there is anything in your child's room that should not be there, anything that would distract them from the Lord? Clean it out! Ask Him for discernment about those things.

If your spouse is under stress, or perhaps even showing signs of depression, pray over their side of the bed, their chair in the dining room, their clothing and personal effects. Pray peace over your spouse through the things they use, the places they sit and recline, the places they work, and the people they are involved with.

At times spiritual housecleaning will require some actual housecleaning as well. This might mean going through the video games or DVDs your children have collected and discarding any that bring an unwanted element into your home. It could mean reviewing the books you have on your bookshelves to see if there are any that need to be thrown out. There could be a piece of artwork, a piece of jewelry like a skull (depicts death), an item of clothing or even some food or drink that needs to be discarded. Doing things like this may generate some heat from others in your home, especially if they are struggling with a growing attitude of rebellion or spiritual drift. It is best to involve your older children in this process.

Our personal choices, the ones we make knowingly or unknowingly, may open the door to wrong influence and influencers. Our parents, grandparents, and extended family members may have patterns of negative influence that need to be conquered and corrected. Your prayers can have a tremendous influence on those. Think for just a moment about a particular pattern or weakness you, your immediate family, your extended family, or even your ancestors have experienced. For example, addictions to alcohol or drugs, sexual sins, chronic illnesses, depression, gossip, slander, laziness, etc. are all potential things that can influence others.

Gambling—and not just casino gambling—but the pursuit of "get-rich-quick" schemes rather than working, constantly buying lottery tickets, excessive card playing or other types of gambling for money can rob a family of its resources and cause devastating financial stress. Your spiritual housecleaning may require extended times of praying over deep seated issues that mar and stain your family's well-being. But it is something that must be done.

HOUSEKEEPING PRAYER

Gracious Lord, as I come to You in prayer now, I ask You to search me and know my heart. Please see if there is anything in me that does not please You (Note: Ps. 139:23-24). I want to confess and forsake all the wrong You reveal to me so I can experience Your forgiveness (Note: Prov. 28:13). Thank You for

Your promise: *"If we confess our sins, he is faithful and just and will forgive us our sins and purify us from all unrighteousness"* (1 Jn. 1:9). I ask Your forgiveness now for all my sins (Note: Ps. 66:18).

As I walk around my home now, Lord, I ask You to cleanse it. I pray for You, O Lord, to break the yoke of bondage, the yoke of fear, the yoke of sickness or disease, the yoke of family conflict, the yoke of deceit, the yoke of generational curses, or *(fill in the blank with a yoke you would like to see the Lord break in your family)* . I ask for forgiveness for any ancestral curses or unbroken vows with the enemy that previously happened in our family or on this property. I repent and renounce any alliances with unacceptable practices displeasing to you Lord and I align only with You. I pray for the healing and restoration of my family and property and for a change from any past destructive and unhealthy family patterns or curses. I ask that none of the sin traits, tendencies toward certain temptations, or *(fill in the blank with a family weakness)* in our family's past or this property's past will be inherited by me, my family, my extended family, or future generations. I pray, rather, that we will *"inherit the kingdom prepared for you from the foundation of the world"* (Matt. 25:34). Your Word promises me: *"You, dear children, are from God and have overcome them, because the one who is in you [the Holy Spirit] is greater than the one who is in the world [the devil]"* (1 Jn. 4:4, brackets added).

As Your child who has been given Your authority (Note: Lk. 10:19), I ask You to cleanse our home and lives of every evil spirit trying to stay here or to claim any authority or ground in this home. We realize we may have opened ourselves up to this influence due to some activity of past or current occupants, visitors, ancestors, or negative patterns that have been passed down (Note: Ex. 20:4). As Your child, Lord, You have given me Your authority: *"Whatever you bind on earth will be bound in heaven, and whatever you loose on earth will be loosed in heaven"* (Matt. 16:19). As Your heir to all the power and authority of Your kingdom (Note: Matt. 25:34), I ask You, Lord, by Your power and authority to identify, rebuke, and remove all evil influences from this home and this property. Fill it with Your Holy Spirit above earth, on earth, and below earth. We ask for Your healing and restoration as You have promised.

Lord God, we are committed to You and Your purposes for our family. We pray for Your freeing Holy Spirit to fill every corner and crevice of our home. We ask You to fill us with the fruit of

Your Spirit: *"But the fruit of the Spirit is love, joy, peace, patience, kindness, goodness, faithfulness, gentleness and self-control"* (Gal. 5:22).

Your Word says, *"Therefore God exalted Him to the highest place and gave Him the name that is above every name, that at the name of Jesus every knee will bow, in heaven and on earth and under the earth, and every tongue confess that Jesus Christ is Lord, to the glory of God the Father"* (Phil. 2:9-11). In the strong name of Jesus, we stand against all the forces and influences of evil and the evil one, and we speak out loud now that You are the rightful King of our home and lives. We give ourselves to You as our Lord, Jesus, and thank You for the power You have given us to command the evil spirits to leave this place (Note: Lk. 10:19). We anoint this home, each room, and this land to be under Your protective care.

ADDITIONAL SCRIPTURES

- *"This is what the Sovereign Lord, the Holy One of Israel, says: 'In repentance and rest is your salvation, in quietness and trust is your strength'"* (Isa. 30:15).

- *"Jesus answered them, 'It is not the healthy who need a doctor, but the sick. I have not come to call the righteous, but sinners to repentance'"* (Lk. 5:31-32).

- *"Repent, then, and turn to God, so that your sins may be wiped out, that times of refreshing may come from the Lord"* (Acts 3:19).

- *"Submit yourselves, then, to God. Resist the devil and he will flee from you. Come near to God and He will come near to you. Wash your hands, you sinners, and purify your hearts, you double-minded ... Humble yourselves before the Lord, and He will lift you up"* (Jas. 4:7,8,10).

- *"'Go,' [Jesus] told him, 'wash in the Pool of Siloam' [this word means 'Sent']. So the man went and washed, and came home seeing"* (Jn. 9:7, brackets added).

- *"But you are a chosen people, a royal priesthood, a holy nation, God's special possession, that you may declare the praises of him who called you out of darkness into his wonderful light"* (1 Pet. 2:9).

LANDSCAPE

Homeowners are generally careful concerning the condition of their property, how the lawn is mowed, how the trees and bushes are tended, and whether or not there are flowers and decorative things on the property. Others, especially within rural areas, have vegetable gardens in which they grow food for consumption as well as for sharing. These, too are an important part of your prayer walk around your property.

Landscape Prayer

Lord, I pray we will experience and live by faith on this land. As You said when You were on earth, *"I haven't seen faith like this in all the land of Israel"* (Matt. 8:10). Lord, I ask that You give me and my family the same kind of faith that Jesus referred to in this passage—a faith held by a Roman centurion that amazed You! Help us to have faith the way Moses did (Note: Heb. 11:27), so that we might dedicate ourselves to following You closer, both individually and as a family, wherever You may lead us.

Creator of everything good, You say, *"children inherited the promised land"* (Ps. 25:13). We look forward with great anticipation to the time when You will come back to set up a new heaven and a new earth (Note: Rev. 21-22), but until that time, let us take care of the land we have underneath our feet right now. I pray, just as our family and friends join us on this land, they will also join us in that Promised Land, heaven.

As Your people said many years ago, so we also say, *"The land is still ours, because we have sought the Lord our God; we sought Him and He has given us rest on every side. So they built and prospered"* (2 Chron. 14:7). Lord, we seek You on this land, thank You for prospering us while we are on this earth, just as You promise.

Lord, I pray Your Word now, *"If my people, who are called by my name, will humble themselves and pray and seek my face and turn from their wicked ways, then will I hear from heaven and will forgive their sin and will heal their land"* (2 Chron. 7:14). I pray for anyone in my family who comes on this land who is not seeking You that they will humble themselves, pray, seek Your face, and turn from their wicked ways so You will hear and heal them. Lord, when we seek You with all our hearts, may You fulfill Your promise to improve, restore, and multiply anything in our lives that we have lost due to not seeking You (Note: Joel 2:25).

Father, while walking the perimeter, anointing the land, praying and dedicating this land to You, I are reminded of Your people walking around Jericho until You gave them a victory over their enemies (Note: Josh. 6). I ask for more faith to trust You as we wait for unanswered prayers and commit to obeying Your voice immediately when we understand what You want us to do. Just as You caused the walls of Jericho to collapse (Note: Josh. 6:20), I ask that You bring down any problem walls within this family. Do Your will in this house and on this land.

Thank You for the variety and beauty of plant life. Thank You for using a garden as an example of Your promise always to guide us, strengthen us, and meet our needs: The Lord will guide you always; he will satisfy your needs in a sun-scorched land and will strengthen your frame. *"You will be like a well-watered garden, like a spring whose waters never fail"* (Isa. 58:11). I pray, Lord, that every person who comes to this garden will be reminded of how You love to meet with us in nature: *"Then the man and his wife heard the sound of the Lord God as he was walking in the garden in the cool of the day"* (Gen. 3:8). May every person who comes into this garden sense Your presence here and may each one find contentment, peace, and the knowledge of You in this garden. In Jesus' name, Amen.

ADDITIONAL SCRIPTURES

- *"God called the dry ground 'land,' and the gathered waters He called 'seas.' And God saw that it was good"* (Gen. 1:10).

- *"Follow justice and justice alone, so that you may live and possess the land the Lord your God is giving you"* (Deut. 16:20).

- *"Trust in the Lord and do good; dwell in the land and enjoy safe pasture"* (Ps. 37:3).

- *"Surely his salvation is near those who fear Him, that His glory may dwell in our land"* (Ps. 85:9).

PART TWO

APPENDIX

PRAYER WALK THROUGH
YOUR HOME
ALPHABETICAL INDEX
OF PRAYERS OVER
HOUSEHOLD OBJECTS

APPENDIX

The Walk

This process will take a significant amount of time, but it should be accomplished in a single day. Set aside a few hours that you can dedicate to this process, then follow through from beginning to end. If you find it is impossible to accomplish this all at one time, do not neglect it for any length of time. Complete it on the next day and be sure to cover each portion of your home until it is complete. Make a commitment to accomplish this in an expedient manner, recognizing that God is able to function outside of a specific time frame, but you are not.

Before you begin your walk, it is important to have forgiven anyone who has offend, hurt, wounded, or misused you in any way. This may be difficult, but it is important. Jesus taught that unless you forgive those who sin against you, the heavenly Father will not forgive you.

It is also important for you to comprehend the significance attached to applying the blood of Jesus as a covering for you, your family, your home, your possessions, your endeavors, and your influence. This goes beyond the legality of your rights before God, and extends to the awareness and protection afforded by Jesus' blood.

"For if you forgive men when they sin against you, your heavenly Father will also forgive you. But if you do not forgive men their sins, your Father will not forgive your sins" (Matt. 6:14-15). It is not that God cannot forgive you, but rather that if forgiving you without you forgiving others, you are bound to that unforgiveness, regardless of what God would do. So, before you begin, start with your own circumstances and pray this prayer of forgiveness and cleansing.

Cleansing and Forgiveness Prayer

Cleanse me from any unrighteous thoughts or acts which I have overlooked in my desire to be Your vessel. I ask forgiveness on behalf of myself, my family, and my ancestors for acts of iniquity, rebellion, sedition, and trespass against You, against one another, and against mankind. I repent and renounce every alliance with these unacceptable practices, religions, alliances, and ideologies. I align myself with You alone, laying aside every weight of self-exaltation, impure motivations, and vain imaginations.

Lord Jesus, please bring to my remembrance anyone I am holding an offense against. Please tell me their names now so I may forgive them permanently. (Spend three minutes of silence, writing down the names the Lord downloads to your memory.)

I ask forgiveness for holding an offense against (those names). Just as You have forgiven me of my sins, I ask You to forgive me for holding bitterness or revenge against them. I release _(name)_ into Your hands and lay aside any resentment I am carrying. I declare a blessing over (name). I repent, and ask You to cleanse me with Your blood. Renew my mind, will, and emotions, and bring them into alignment with Yours. Guard my heart and soul so that I do not develop a root of bitterness. Thank You Lord, for Your grace. (Note: Matt 6:12,14,15; Mark 11:25; Lk. 17:3-4; Jn. 20:23).

Lord, I ask You to cleanse this land and its surroundings, this house and all of the objects within it from anything or any activity that has taken place here that dishonors or displeases You. Bring to my memory anything I may have knowledge of or unknowingly participated in that was against Your wishes. Reveal anything that is here which invites darkness, evil, or falsehood to have a place of recognition. I consecrate this house and this property and all of the objects within it as dedicated to preserve righteousness and honor You, my Lord and my God.

Cleanse me from of all this by the blood of Jesus. Cover this dwelling and its inhabitants with Jesus' blood covenant covering, and fill us with your Holy Spirit, so that in every place this cleansing will be obvious, and Your presence will be experienced.

In Jesus' holy name, I pray—amen.

APPENDIX

What follows is an alphabetical arrangement of prayers that can be spoken over various objects in and around your home. These prayers draw special attention to specific objects which have influence on the feelings, thoughts, and activities of you and your family. It is a reference guide to prayer which can be used again and again as need arises. I pray it will bless and encourage you as you speak blessings over your home and family.

A

ACTIVITY CALENDAR

Gracious Lord, thank You for all opportunities scheduled on this calendar. Give me the good sense to turn down those You do not want me or our family to attend, and to schedule only those events You approve. I pray Your blessing by clearly showing us how to budget our time according to Your will and plan for our lives. Thank You for these activities listed on this calendar.

- *"Show me, Lord, my life's end and the number of my days; let me know how fleeting my life is. You have made my days a mere handbreadth; the span of my years is as nothing before you"* (Ps. 39:4,5).

- *"The Lord makes firm the steps of the one who delights in him"* (Ps. 37:23).

- *"In their hearts humans plan their course, but the Lord establishes their steps"* (Prov. 16:9).

ANGELS

Thank You, Lord, for Your promise to my family and me that *"The Angel of the Lord encamps around those who fear him, and he delivers them"* (Ps. 34:7).

Thank You, heavenly Father, that You give Your angels direction to protect us and also to hear directly from You as to how they can help our family best:

- *"For I tell you that in heaven their angels are always in the presence of my heavenly Father"* (Matt. 18:10 NLT).

- *"Angels are always looking at You and are eager to do Your slightest bidding for our good"* (Heb. 1:7).

- *"Praise Him, all His angels; praise Him all His hosts"* (Ps. 148:2 NASB).

I pray that every time we see this picture of angels that it will remind us of how Your angels are guarding our family and that You personally are directing them to do good for us.

- *"For he will order his angels to protect you wherever you go. They will hold you up with their hands so you won't even hurt your foot on a stone"* (Ps. 91:11-12 NLT).

ART/DESIGN/CRAFTS

Lord of Creation, because art showcases Your beauty and depth, I pray You will give every person who looks at this artwork a glimpse of Your creative genius and Spirit. May they understand and appreciate the true meaning behind the art that is Your creation. I ask that it reflect You as Creator, Redeemer and Friend. Bless each one in my family, my extended family, and my friends who see this picture by reminding us that every event in the universe finds its reality and makes sense in You alone (Note: Rom. 8:28). Anoint all who see this picture so it reflects the truth of Your Word, *"No eye has seen, no ear has heard, no mind has conceived what God has prepared for those who love him"* (1 Cor. 2:9). Let this artwork reveal people's hearts to them (Note: Lk. 2:35) and what they are drawn to—and if there are things in their lives that do not showcase Your beauty, please remove them. Thank You that in a very real sense, the world in which we live is a reflection of You.

Thank You, Lord, that we can discern the difference between right and wrong, between good and bad. You have revealed through the Ten Commandments how we are to live (Note: Ex. 20:1-21) and to love one another. I pray my family will use Your Word when making decisions, because You tell us: *"Do not merely listen to the word, and so deceive yourselves. Do what it says"* (Jas. 1:22).

I also thank You for the creativity we experience as we are designing, drafting, or crafting projects. We know we are reflecting You and Your creativity when we imagine things that are not yet visible, or piece things together in fresh and interesting ways. These God-given gifts are totally from You and spring from Your beauty. Let the things we design bring glory to You, O God, for we are designed in Your image. May everything we create align with Your Word, especially where we learn these promises:

- *"He made known to us the mystery of his will according to his good pleasure, which he purposed in Christ, to be put into effect when the times reach their fulfillment—to bring unity to all things in heaven and on earth under Christ"* (Eph. 1:9-10).

- *"Every good and perfect gift is from above, coming down from the Father of the heavenly lights, who does not change like shifting shadows"* (Jas. 1:17).

- *"We look at this Son and see the God who cannot be seen. We look at this Son and see God's original purpose in everything created. For everything, absolutely everything, above and below, visible and invisible, rank after rank after rank of angels—everything got started in him and finds its purpose in him"* (Col. 1:15-16, MSG).

- *"Yes, everything else is worthless when compared with the infinite value of knowing Christ Jesus my Lord. For his sake I have discarded everything else, counting it all as garbage, so that I could gain Christ"* (Phil. 3:8 NLT).

- *"And I have filled him with the Spirit of God, with wisdom, with understanding, with knowledge and with all kinds of skills—to make artistic designs for work in gold, silver and bronze, to cut and set stones, to work in wood, and to engage in all kinds of crafts"* (Ex. 31:3-5).

- *"He has filled them with skill to do all kinds of work as engravers, designers, embroiderers in blue, purple and scarlet yarn and fine linen, and weavers—all of them skilled workers and designers"* (Ex. 35:35).

- *"Therefore since we are God's offspring, we should not think that the divine being is like gold or silver or stone—an image made by human design and skill"* (Acts 17:29).

B

BED/SHEETS/PILLOWS

Lord, I pray Your blessing on everyone who will lie down on this bed, use these sheets, and lay their head on these pillows.

As we lie down on this bed to rest, let us find our true rest and peace in trusting You: *"You will keep in perfect peace all who trust in you, all whose thoughts are fixed on you!"* (Isa. 26:3 NLT). You say, *"Rest in the Lord and wait patiently for Him"* (Ps. 37:7 NASB). Thank You for the rest You give us and for being the God of all comfort to us (Note: 2 Cor. 1:3). I praise You for the comfort and rest we gain while we sleep on this bed, and I ask Your blessing on all who rest here.

- *"I will lie down and sleep in peace, for you alone, O Lord, make me dwell in safety"* (Ps. 4:8).

- *"In vain you rise early and stay up late, toiling for food to eat— for he grants sleep to those he loves"* (Ps. 127:2).

- *"I will pour out my Spirit on all people. Your sons and daughters will prophesy, your old men will dream dreams, your young men will see visions"* (Joel 2:28).

- *"When there is a prophet among you, I, The Lord, reveal myself to them in visions, I speak to them in dreams"* (Num. 12:6).

- *"At Gibeon the Lord appeared to Solomon during the night in a dream, and God said, 'Ask for whatever you want me to give you'"* (1 Kgs. 3:5).

- *"An angel of the Lord appeared to him in a dream and said, 'Joseph, son of David, do not be afraid to take Mary home as your wife, because what is conceived in her is from the Holy Spirit'"* (Matt. 1:20).

You may even want to write these verses on a 3 x 5 card and place it under the mattress or under the bed as a special prayer for the person who uses the bed.

BIRDS

As I look at these birds, I am reminded of Your promise to provide for my family's every *need*.

- *Consider the ravens: They do not sow or reap, they have no storeroom or barn; yet God feeds them. And how much more valuable you are than birds!* (Lk. 12:24)

Thank You that we are made in Your image and are more valuable to You than any of Your other creatures. Thank You that You have provided this home for my family, provided our food, our water, and every good thing that is in our lives. Help us to remember it was all created by You and is a gift from You (Note: Jas. 1:17).

Thank You that You use the birds to teach me of Your nature. *"Just ask the animals, and they will teach you. Ask the birds of the sky, and they will tell you"* (Job 12:7 NLT).

Thank You for the birds that sing. *"The birds nest beside the streams and sing among the branches of the trees"* (Ps. 104:12 NLT). Singing birds provide so much happiness in our lives. As the birds sing in praise of You, I want to do the same. *"Sing joyfully to the Lord, you righteous; it is fitting for the upright to praise him"* (Ps. 33:1).

As we see birds each day, remind us about how detailed your knowledge of us is and how much You love us, like You say, *"Are you not much more valuable than [birds]?"* (Matt. 6:26), so we have no need to *worry!*

BLANKETS

As members of my family find warmth and comfort under this blanket, I pray that we will remember we can only be truly comforted in times of trouble or stress by You. Let us trust in Your protection, for You are the source of all comfort (Note:

2 Cor. 1:3). Help us find our warmth and comfort by praying about every situation, need, or struggle we have because You tell us: *"Give all your worries and cares to God, for he cares about you"* (1 Peter 5:7 NLT).

I pray You will remind those who use this blanket as it covers and warms them, You cover and warm their souls and spirits, and they can find great comfort in knowing: *"Blessed is he whose transgressions are forgiven, whose sins are covered"* (Ps. 32:1). Thank You that we are able to have our shortcomings  and sins forgiven by Your forgiveness through the mercy and grace You give us. Thank You for blanketing us with the security of Your love (Note: Eph. 3:18,19). I pray that every person who sees or uses this blanket will remember the warmth, security, and wonderful happiness life can have because of Your love. Use this blanket, Lord, as a physical reminder of the spiritual reality that our sins are covered by Your love so that we can be secure in our eternal relationship with You.

BOATS

Lord, as I look at this picture of a boat, I recall an incident in Your earthly *life*.

> *"[Your disciples] had rowed three or four miles when suddenly they saw Jesus walking on the water toward the boat. They were terrified, but he called out to them, "Don't be afraid. I am here!" Then they were eager to let him in the boat, and immediately they arrived at their destination!"* (Jn. 6:19-21 NLT, brackets added).

Thank You that You control the weather, You can walk on water … You can do anything: *"Is anything too hard for the Lord?"* (Gen. 18:14). I pray that this picture of a boat will remind everyone who sees it that You are God—able to do anything. I pray as people see the boat they will invite You into their lives so they can reach the destination You have planned for them.

BOOKS/READING MATERIAL

Lord, I pray that the reading material in our home—books, magazines, catalogues, or on a screen, will be appropriate. Thank You that the Bible is Your instruction book for our lives because You tell us:

※ *"The instructions of the Lord are perfect, reviving the soul. The decrees of the Lord are trustworthy, making wise the simple. The commandments of the Lord are right, bringing joy to the heart. The commands of the Lord are clear, giving insight for living. Reverence for the Lord is pure, lasting forever. The laws of the Lord are true; each one is fair."* (Ps. 19:7-9 NLT).

Thank You for the desires that have been written in Your Word: *"My son, if you accept my words and store up my commands within you… For the Lord gives wisdom, and from his mouth come knowledge and understanding… Then you will understand what is right and just and fair— every good path"* (Prov. 2:1, 6, 9).

As we read, help us be able to memorize Scripture on a daily basis. Help us remember to turn to Your Word for life instructions. May the things we read and the reading material in our home refresh us and be a reflection of Your Word and Your life for us. Let us be careful about the things we see,

hear, and say in return: *"May these words of my mouth and this meditation of my heart be pleasing in your sight, Lord, my Rock and my Redeemer"* (Ps. 19:14).

Protect our minds as we read, so we meditate on things that are true, noble, right, pure, lovely, admirable, excellent, and praiseworthy (Note: Phil. 4:8). If our reading takes us beyond these attributes, we ask You to remove the impressions they leave from our minds and hearts, so that we may remain pure before You.

- *"Fix these words of mine in your hearts and minds; tie them as symbols on your hands and bind them on your foreheads"* (Deut. 11:18).

- *"When I applied my mind to know wisdom and to observe the labor that is done on earth—people getting no sleep day or night—then I saw all that God has done. No one can comprehend what goes on under the sun. Despite all their efforts to search it out, no one can discover its meaning. Even if the wise claim they know, they cannot really comprehend it"* (Eccl. 8:16-17).

- *"You will keep in perfect peace those whose minds are steadfast, because they trust in you"* (Isa. 26:3).

- *"Love the Lord your God with all your heart and with all your soul and with all your mind and with all your strength"* (Mk. 12:30).

BUILDINGS/STRUCTURES

Lord, You are the Architect and Builder of the world. You gave detailed plans to Moses for the building of the tabernacle, and prophetic instructions to David for the building of the temple. You instructed that the best materials be used and gave details of each structure to its most minute part, so that Your excellence would be seen by the worshipper. I pray Your richest blessing on the people in these buildings, these shops, residential buildings, or _(fill in the blank with a building as well as the building's structures)_ .

You are the Builder of our lives, and You say Your *"solid foundation stands firm, sealed with this inscription: The Lord knows who are his"* (2 Tim. 2:19). I pray You will draw all of these people in these buildings to You. You promise, *"Come near to God and he will come near to you"* (Jas. 4:8). I ask that I will consistently use Your blueprints to build a life graced by Your richest blessings. Thank You for this promise: *"For we are God's fellow workers; you are God's field, God's building ... For no one can lay any foundation other than the one already laid, which is Jesus Christ"* (1 Cor. 3:9,11).

I pray You will bless my family and me as we build our lives based on Jesus Christ as our only foundation, remembering that we are Your earthly building and builders. *"Lord our God, all the abundance we have for building You a temple for Your Holy Name comes from Your hand, and all of it belongs to You"* (1 Chron. 29:16).

Just as builders use plans, let us use the Bible for our plans for the future (Note: Ps. 19:7-14). May every activity in these buildings bring You honor and glory, and may You bless each person who uses these buildings or structures. Use them in a way that accomplishes Your purposes through these buildings.

- *"The day for building your walls will come, the day for extending your boundaries"* (Mic. 7:11).

- *"He raises the poor from the dust and lifts the needy from the ash heap; he seats them with princes and has them inherit a throne of honor. For the foundations of the earth are the Lord's; on them he has set the world"* (1 Sam. 2:8).

- *"Where were you when I laid the earth's foundation?"* (Job 38:4).

- *"Righteousness and justice are the foundation of your throne; love and faithfulness go before you"* (Ps. 89:14).

BUSHES/TREES

Lord, as I see these bushes, it reminds me of how You spoke to Moses: *"There the angel of the Lord appeared to him in a blazing fire from the middle of a bush. Moses stared in amazement. Though the bush was engulfed in flames, it didn't burn up. 'This is amazing,' Moses said to himself. 'Why isn't that bush burning up? I must go see it.' When the Lord saw Moses coming to take a closer look, God called to him from the middle of the bush, 'Moses! Moses!' 'Here I am!' Moses replied"* (Ex. 3:2-4 NLT).

As You called to Moses from the burning bush, I pray that You will give us eyes to see where You are and to respond to You every day as You direct us. May these bushes remind us constantly of how You are a communicating God and how much You love to show us Your will and ways.

I ask especially that these bushes will remind us of how much You desire our lives to bear good fruit or good deeds, encouraging others to know Christ, *"By their fruit you will recognize them. Do people pick grapes from thorn bushes, or figs from thistles?"* (Matt. 7:16).

May each time we see these trees be a reminder to us of how You cause us to grow, give us strength, and make us like great oaks You have planted. I pray that my family and I may stand strong and true like trees before You, that our roots will go deep into the soil of Your love and life. Thank You,

Lord, that You love to give strength and life to my family, my extended family, our friends, and me.

- "To all who mourn in Israel, he will give a crown of beauty for ashes, a joyous blessing instead of mourning, festive praise instead of despair. In their righteousness they will be like great oaks that the Lord has planted for his own glory" (Isa. 61:3 NLT).

- "Blessed are those who trust in the Lord and have made the Lord their hope and confidence. They are like trees planted along a riverbank, with roots that reach deep into the water. Such trees are not bothered by the heat or worried by long months of drought. Their leaves stay green, and they never stop producing fruit" (Jer. 17:6-8 NLT).

- "The Lord God made all kinds of trees grow out of the ground—trees that were pleasing to the eye and good for food. In the middle of the garden were the tree of life and the tree of the knowledge of good and evil" (Gen. 2:9).

- "Whoever has ears, let them hear what the Spirit says to the churches. To the one who is victorious, I will give the right to eat from the tree of life, which is in the paradise of God" (Rev. 2:7).

- "Blessed are those who wash their robes, that they may have the right to the tree of life and may go through the gates into the city" (Rev. 22:14).

C

CANDLES

May every member of my family—and the friends who use these candles—be reminded to walk in Your light because *"Your Word is a lamp to my feet, and a light for my path"* (Ps. 119:105).

Thank You, Lord, for who You are: *"You light a lamp for me. The Lord, my God, lights up my darkness"* (Ps. 18:28 NLT). We live in a dark world, so I pray that every person who sees this candle will remember the position You have given them to light their world.

You say, *"No one lights a lamp and then puts it under a basket. Instead, a lamp is placed on a stand, where it gives light to everyone in the house. In the same way, let your good deeds shine out for all to see, so that everyone will praise your heavenly Father"* (Matt. 5:15-16 NLT). May You use my family and my influence to touch other people in a godly way, always pointing back to You.

Just as this candle gives light, I pray we will walk in the light of Your Word so we can have a sense of belonging and relationship with You: *"But if we walk in the light, as he is in the light, we have fellowship with one another, and the blood of Jesus, his Son, purifies us from all sin"* (1 Jn. 1:7). May each person who uses these candles find the incredible blessing of friendship with You.

- *"I will praise the Lord, who counsels me; even at night my heart instructs me"* (Ps. 16:7).

- *"For you were once darkness, but now you are light in the Lord. Live as children of light (for the fruit of the light consists in all goodness, righteousness and truth)"* (Eph. 5:8-9).

- *"To open their eyes and turn them from darkness to light, and from the power of Satan to God, so that they may receive forgiveness of sins and a place among those who are sanctified by faith in me"* (Acts 26:18).

- *"For there is nothing hidden that will not be disclosed, and nothing concealed that will not be known or brought out into the open"* (Lk. 8:17).

Note: See also Eph. 1:18, Ps. 23:3, Ps. 36:9, Ps. 43:3, Ps. 84:11, Ps. 97:11, Matt. 4:22, Jn. 1:5, Jn. 3:21, Jn. 8:12, and 2 Cor. 4:6.

CARS

Dear Lord, I anoint this car as I pray out loud that everyone who rides in or drives it will be safe and protected.

Lord, You are our protector: *"God is our refuge and strength, always ready to help in times of trouble"* (Ps. 46:1 NLT). Please surround our car with Your strong angels, and place a hedge of protection around it to keep us safe in traffic. You tell us, *"Regarding the angels, he says, 'He sends his angels like the winds, his servants like flames of fire'"* (Heb. 1:7). Please stir our consciousness when we travel into areas we should not go or into places of danger of which we are unaware. We ask if there is something not working properly You will alert us so we will have it inspected and repaired. We especially pray that we will not endanger our family because of a mechanical problem, because You want us to love one another by our actions and not just words (Note: 1 Jn. 3:16-18).

We pray we will drive efficiently, using our time and fuel in a manner that would be pleasing to You and help bring additional people to know You. We want to drive as though You are seated in the vehicle with us, because You really are. We ask if someone is riding without a seat belt that You will remind them or help us to remind them to buckle up.

Lord, if You want us to go to certain places in order to influence people or be surrounded by other Christians, we pray You will bring that to mind so we can follow Your plan for our lives.

CHAIRS

Thank You for providing chairs where we can sit, chat, and rest together with friends and family. We know You bring with You comfort, peace, rest, and relaxation. Thank You for Your promise to my family, my extended family, my friends, and me that when we open the door of our hearts, You say, *"I will come in, and we will share a meal together as friends"* (Rev. 3:20 NLT).

We invite You to sit with us at a table as we enjoy a meal, talk, play a board game, or have camaradarie together. We ask You

to direct our conversations. Thank You that You love to be involved in every aspect of our lives. Bless each person who sits in these chairs. We pray they will feel Your presence as they rest and recline in them, that You will bring restoration as we wait on You (Note: Isa. 40:31).

Lord, we are so grateful for the privilege of sitting down and sharing a meal with others. When we do so in these chairs, let our conversation be holy, uplifting, and edifying to ourselves and others. Let our home always be open and welcome to any guests You see fit to send our way, so that we can share Your love, fellowship, and laughter with others as we use these chairs.

- *"Your love has given me great joy and encouragement, because you, brother, have refreshed the hearts of the Lord's people"* (Phm. 1:7).

- *"But if we walk in the light, as he is in the light, we have fellowship with one another, and the blood of Jesus, his Son, purifies us from all sin"* (1 Jn. 1:7).

- *"Dear friends, let us love one another, for love comes from God. Everyone who loves has been born of God and knows God. Whoever does not love does not know God, because God is love"* (1 Jn. 4:7-8).

- *"They devoted themselves to the apostles' teaching and to fellowship, to the breaking of bread and to prayer"* (Acts 2:42).

CHESS SET/BOARD GAMES

Thank You, Lord, for this chess set and the board games we enjoy as a family and with friends. Just as we preplan our moves in chess, checkers, or our favorite board game, we know

You have a great plan for our lives: *"'For I know the plans I have for you,' declares the Lord, 'plans to prosper you and not to harm you, plans to give you hope and a future'"* (Jer. 29:11-12).

I ask You to reveal Your earthly plan for my family and me in ways we can see and understand. Direct the steps of our lives so we will consistently be moving according to Your will. We ask Your blessing and anointing on our family, extended family, and friends who will play our chess set and board games, and we ask You to remind us of Your plans for us as we play.

- *"The Lord makes firm the steps of the one who delights in him"* (Ps. 37:23).

- *"You make known to me the path of life; you will fill me with joy in your presence, with eternal pleasures at your right hand"* (Ps. 16:11).

CHILDREN'S BEDS

As ___*(children's names)*___ lies in bed, I pray they will have peaceful, sweet dreams. Protect them from bad dreams or evil influences that will disturb, wound, or hurt their heart, mind, or soul. Grant ___(children's names)___) restful, refreshing, and invigorating sleep. You promised that, *"the Lord is faithful, and He will strengthen and protect you from the evil one"* (2 Thess. 3:3).

Cause ___(children's names)___ to relax underneath the warm blankets and to feel secure, comforted, and loved by You.

Lord Jesus, as they lay down to go to sleep, and recall the day's events, I pray they will rest peacefully. You have said, *"You will keep in perfect peace all whose minds are stayed on You, because they trust in You"* (Isa. 26:3 NLT); and *"When you lie down, you will not be afraid; when you lie down, your sleep will be sweet"* (Prov. 3:24). As the memories of the day are recounted, help them  remember to share every thought with You. Teach them, O God, that they can pray anywhere, at anytime, about anything.

Please comfort my children and allow them to clear their heads of all thoughts, worries, concerns, and emotions that would keep them from having restful sleep. Please give them Your peace and love to allow them to rest through the entire night and to awake refreshed in the morning. Help quiet their minds for sleep, focusing on the Word of God, thanking You for the good things that happened to them today. Fill their hearts with gratitude, courage, and expectancy for a bright new day when they awaken.

- *"When you lie down, you will not be afraid; when you lie down, your sleep will be sweet"* (Prov. 3:24).

- *"Hope deferred makes the heart sick, but a longing fulfilled is a tree of life"* (Prov. 13:12).

- *"In the last days, God says, I will pour out my Spirit on all people. Your sons and daughters will prophesy, your young men will see visions, your old men will dream dreams"* (Acts 2:17).

- *"In peace I will lie down and sleep, for you alone, Lord, make me dwell in safety"* (Ps. 4:8).

CHILD'S DRESSER

Lord, I pray You will bless my child and use the items in and on this dresser to help my child think of Your great love for them. As they pull clothing from these drawers, may they remember to *"clothe [themselves] with the presence of the Lord Jesus Christ"* (Rom. 13:14 NLT, brackets added) and with *"compassion, kindness, humility, gentleness, and patience"* (Col.

3:12). When they look at special items on top of the dresser, may they remember the special memories associated with this memorabilia. Help them create special memories with You, Lord, by inviting You to be a part of their lives as they go out to play, work, socialize, or hang out with the family and friends. I ask, O God, that You will become my children's best friend, and let them constantly know of Your deep, eternal love for them. Give them the Spirit of wisdom and revelation so that they may know You better (Note: Eph. 1:17).

CHILDREN'S BLINDS/WINDOW COVERINGS

Lord, I ask out loud for You to provide a clear view through this window for my children to see Your handiwork in nature. Lord, thank You that we can look out at the world You created and reflect on the variety and depth of Your creative genius.

Lord, every night these blinds or window coverings hide the darkness outside from our view. Help *(children's names)* and me to recognize where there may be darkness in our lives. I pray that the schemes of the enemy will be revealed every time he tries to lie, cheat, or steal a positive life from my children. I stand in alliance with You, O Lord, against any enemy attacks targeted at my children, and I say that a spirit of fear will have no place in his or her life. *"For God has not given us a spirit of fear, but of power and love and a sound mind"* (2 Tim. 1:7).

Strengthen my child's faith in You, Lord, to be their Defender. Thank You for being our great Protector.

Thank You, Lord, that You say, *"The light shines in the darkness, and the darkness can never overcome it"* (Jn. 1:5). I pray that ___(children's names)___ will live in

the light of Your truth; help them to rise above the criticism of others and be more concerned about what You already know about them—and how much You love them. Thank You, Lord, that the God who knows us best loves us the most. May they only be concerned with pleasing You because You tell us, *"So then, we make it our aim ... to please Him"* (2 Cor. 5:9). Enable my children at every age to grow stronger in You and say, *"The Lord is my light and my salvation; whom shall I fear? The Lord is the strength of my life; of whom shall I be afraid?"* (Ps. 27:1). Let my child stand on Your promise that You make Your light shine in our hearts to give us the light of knowledge of God's glory displayed in the face of Christ (Note: Col. 4:6).

I speak Your blessing over my children as they look through this window. Every time they look through these window coverings or blinds, may they be reminded how bright Your love shines on their life and how You have overcome all darkness!

CHILD'S CLOSET

Lord, we read in Scripture, *"What matters is not your outer appearance—the styling of your hair, the jewelry you wear, the cut of your clothes—but your inner disposition. Cultivate inner beauty, the gentle, gracious kind that God delights in"* (1 Pet. 3:3-4 MSG). I pray as my children put on clothing from this closet they will be more concerned with wearing a gentle and quiet spirit.

Since what we wear reflects our character, I pray my children will reflect a strong, Christ-filled character to the world through the clothes they choose to wear. But most of all, let them be robed in righteousness (Note: Isa. 61:10). Father, let them put on the full armor of God each day, so they can stand against the devils' schemes (Note: Eph. 6:10-18). Let them wear the belt of truth, the breastplate of righteousness, shoes of peace, the shield of faith, the helmet of salvation, and the sword of the spirit. With this armor on, let my children stand firm and resist the enemy. Let them recognize that this is Your armor they are wearing: thus they will trust You in the battles they will face. Remind them that the battle is not theirs but Yours (Note: 2 Chron. 20).

CHILD'S MIRROR

As my children look at their faces in this mirror, let them see themselves as You see them. When their spirits are out of sync with You, let them run to You quickly to shape and mold them.

We read in Your Word: *"Anyone who listens to the word but does not do what it says is like a man who looks at his face in a mirror and, after looking at himself, goes away and immediately forgets what he looks like. But the man who looks intently into the perfect law that gives freedom, and continues to do this, not forgetting what he has heard, but doing it—he will be blessed in what he does"* (Jas. 1:23-25).

Let my children always look into Your perfect law and thus walk in the freedom it brings. Let them not forget what they have heard or read in Your Word but act on it and be blessed in what they do.

Dear Lord, as my children look in the mirror, help them each see the beautiful child You created (Note: Jn. 1:3-5) and how distinctive they are (Note: Ps. 139:13-14). Help them see that You, God, have given them unique talents that will fill their hearts with joy. Help me as a parent to recognize and encourage the development of these talents, because You say, *"Therefore encourage one another and build each other up, just as in fact you are doing"* (1 Thess. 5:11).

May my children be encouraged at what they see in the mirror today, Lord. As they look upon their reflections, bring to mind, *"As water reflects the face, so one's life reflects the heart"* (Prov. 27:19).

Lord, I speak out loud and ask You to please bless __(children's names)__ as (he/she) looks in the mirror today and every day, and enable (him/her) to see a beautiful, loving, light-filled child created by God.

CHILD'S DESK

Lord Jesus, as my children study at this desk, I pray they will enjoy it and do their schoolwork with an eye toward Your rewards (Note: Col. 3:23-24). You remind us, *"Study to show yourself approved to God, a workman that is not ashamed"* (2 Tim.

2:15). May each child learn valuable lessons from their studies, preparing them for the wonderful future You have for them (Note: Jer. 29:11-13). I pray they will develop quality character at

this desk as well—character traits like sticking to a task until it is completed, disciplining themselves to study subjects they do not particularly enjoy, developing a thirst for knowledge, and applying their new knowledge in real-life situations. May You bless my children as they study at this desk, and may each one study to the best of (his/her) ability. Help them focus and concentrate. Help them to make good use of their time, and remove any distractions.

I pray they will develop a good self-image as they complete homework and projects at this desk. I pray *(children's names)* will find their true identity in You. Help them understand their true worth in Your eyes and consider Your great love for them; that they are truly children of the King of the universe—royalty! May they be given a spirit of wisdom and revelation in understanding their unique gifts from You, appreciating them, and using them at this desk.

Enable them to see themselves the way You do, understanding that You give clarity, wisdom, security, purpose, and true lasting worth.

> *"The fear of the Lord is the beginning of wisdom; all who follow his precepts have good understanding. To him belongs eternal praise"* (Ps. 111:10).

CITY SKYLINE

As I look at this picture of my city's skyline, I pray Your grace and protection over our city. Your Word says, *"You will be blessed in the city and blessed in the country"* (Deut. 28:3). Bless every person in this city with a lasting relationship with You, as well as a fulfilling life, protection, and a sense of Your peace, presence, and safety. Bless those who I see in the office buildings, that the workers there would become aware of You and Your presence. Bless the businesses in those buildings, and all the righteous businesses throughout our city, that they would be profitable and operate with integrity. Protect our city from crime and degradation, and protect those who fight against such things. Protect our police force, our fire fighters, our first responders and our other civil servants who make our city safer and cleaner. Protect the ministries located here and cause them to let the light of the Gospel come forth here. Thank You for this city skyline. May it constantly remind us of how You are Lord of our city. We pray You will bless our city beyond all we could ask or imagine (Note: Eph. 3:20). We plead the blood of Jesus over our city and ask You to bless it with Your presence and peace.

CLOCKS

Lord, as I look at this clock, I am reminded of how quickly time flies. I pray for every person who looks at this clock, that You will *"Teach us to number our days aright, that we may gain a heart of wisdom"* (Ps. 90:12). Help us to use our time wisely and in a manner in which You would like us to spend it. You instructed us to, *"Be very careful, then, how you live—not as unwise but as wise, making the most of your time, because the days are evil. Therefore do not be foolish, but understand what the Lord's will is"* (Eph. 5:15-17).

Thank You that Your times are always <u>right</u>. *"The Lord will send rain at the proper time from his rich treasury in the heavens and will bless all the work you do"* (Deut. 28:12 NLT).

Our lives are brief and each day is precious. Help us do the most good we can for people as long as we can. Give us insight how to serve others, whether taking a meal to a shut-in family member or friend, or providing much-needed help financially, physically, emotionally, spiritually, or __(fill in the blank with a good deed you or your family can do)__ .  As we see this clock every day, may it remind us to love and serve You with the life we have now. May we celebrate each day as a precious gift.

- *"This is the day the Lord has made; let us rejoice and be glad in it"* (Ps. 118:24).

As we awaken to the sound of our alarm clocks each morning, I ask You to remind us that You want to give us a better, fuller, and happier life than we would ever ask or imagine (Note: Eph. 3:20). We ask You to order our days and remind us each morning how short-lived they are, so we will grow in wisdom (Note: Ps. 90:12 NLT). I pray Your blessing and anointing on my family, in Your time—for there is a time for everything under heaven (Note: Eccl. 3:1-8).

CLOUDS

Lord, I thank You for the beautiful clouds that bring life-giving rain and comforting shelter from the heat of the sun's rays. As I consider these clouds, I am reminded how You say in Your Word, *"Therefore, since we are surrounded by such a great cloud of witnesses, let us throw off everything that hinders and the sin that so easily entangles, and let us run with perseverance the race marked out for us"* (Heb. 12:1). Give us strength to run the race well so we may be witnesses for You.

I pray that every time we see clouds they will remind us of Your promise: *"I will bless them ... I will send down showers in season; there will be showers of blessing"* (Ezek. 34:26). May we be happy, praise-filled, thankful people as we recount to You all the wonderful blessings You shower on our lives.

   "I'm putting my rainbow in the clouds, a sign of the covenant between me and the Earth. From now on, when I form a cloud over the Earth and the rainbow appears in the cloud, I'll remember my covenant between me and you and everything living, that never again will floodwaters destroy all life. When

the rainbow appears in the cloud, I'll see it and remember the eternal covenant between God and everything living, every last living creature on Earth" (Gen. 9:12 MSG).

- "Can you get the attention of the clouds, and commission a shower of rain? Can you take charge of the lightning bolts and have them report to you for orders?" (Job 38:34 MSG)

- "Open up, heavens, and rain. Clouds, pour out buckets of my goodness! Loosen up, earth, and bloom salvation; sprout right living. I, God, generate all this" (Isa. 45:8 MSG).

- "By day the Lord went ahead of them in a pillar of cloud to guide them on their way and by night in a pillar of fire to give them light, so that they could travel by day or night" (Ex. 13:21).

- "I will bless them ... I will send down showers in season; there will be showers of blessing" (Ezek. 34:26).

COAT/HAT RACKS

Thank You, Lord, for this coat rack. Remind us each time we use it that hats and coats provide an outer layer of protection for our bodies and our inner clothing. Just as was said of the godly woman in Proverbs 31, I pray it will be true of my family and me. *"When it snows, she has no fear for her household; for all of them are clothed in scarlet"* (Prov. 31:21).

Thank You for Your firm grip on my life. *"With a strong hand, God grabs my shirt. He grips me by the collar of my coat"* (Job 30:18 NLT). Thank You for holding us tightly and for keeping us *protected*.

COLORS*

- **Red represents wisdom, anointing, power and the blood of Jesus.** *"But if we walk in the light, as he is in the light, we have fellowship with one another, and the blood of Jesus, his Son, purifies us from all sin"* (1 Jn. 1:7).

Thank You, Lord, that red signifies the blood of Jesus. Thank You, Jesus, for dying on the cross and shedding Your blood for my sins. Thank You that Your blood is still purifying my life today.

- **Blue represents revelation, communion, and heaven.** *"... our fellowship is with the Father and with his Son, Jesus Christ ... God is light; in him there is no darkness at all ... But if we walk in the light, as he is in the light, we have fellowship with one another ..."* (1 Jn. 1:3b, 4b, 7)

Thank You, Lord, that You reveal Yourself in holy light that draws my family and me into the circle of Your fellowship (communion) where we find joy among those who walk in Your love.

- **Purple is the color of royalty and represents Divine authority.** *"The soldiers twisted together a crown of thorns and put it on his head. They clothed him in a purple robe and went up to him again and again, saying, 'Hail, king of the Jews!' And they struck him in the face"* (Jn. 19:2-3).

Thank You, Lord Jesus, that You were willing to suffer a cruel death on the cross for our salvation. I yield to you, my King of kings and the Lord of lords and ask you to reign in my home. *"On His robe and on His thigh He has this name written: 'King of Kings and Lord of Lords'"* (Rev. 19:16)

- **White represents righteousness, holiness, and light.** *"Jesus ... was transfigured before them. His face shone like the sun, and his clothes became as white as the light"* (Matt. 17:1-2).

Lord, as Your appearance changed, I pray I, too, will change to be more like You as I daily submit my life to You, Your Word, prayer, and the Holy Spirit (Note: 2 Cor. 3:18).

- **Gold is one of the most valuable items on earth. It represents purity, glory, and holiness.** In heaven, *"The great street of the city was of pure gold, like transparent glass"* (Rev. 21:21).

Lord, I pray that my family and I will embrace Your eternal values because what we value here on this earth as most precious will be of little value in heaven. Allow our holiness to shine before others like the radiance of pure gold.

- **Silver represents redemption, grace, and purification.** Silver must be purified before it can have value. Silver has been used as a value measurement for money since ancient times. *"The crucible for silver and the furnace for gold, but the Lord tests the heart"* (Prov. 17:3).

Lord, when I feel the heat of trials, I know You are bringing greater purity to my life, so I thank you for allowing me to be strong in the face of difficulties.

- **Green represents growth and prosperity.** *"He makes me lie down in green pastures, he leads me beside quiet waters"* (Ps. 23:2).

Thank You, Lord, that You cause me to be refreshed in green, restful *places.*

- **Yellow represents hope and the mind.** *"… Those who live in accordance with the Spirit have their minds set on what the Spirit desires. The mind of sinful man is death, but the mind controlled by the Spirit is life and peace"* (Rom 8:5b-6a NIV).

Thank You, Lord, that You have given me the mind of Christ (1 Cor. 2:16) so I may live in the full confidence (hope) of my faith in You.

- **Pink represents childlikeness and the love of God.** *"… Anyone who will not receive the kingdom of God like a little child will never enter it"* (Lk. 18:17)

As a child would trust You, I present myself to You, Lord, with total dependence on Your love and strength. Thank You for Your amazing *love*.

- **Orange represents perseverance, the resolve to never yield to the enemy.** *"Watch your life and doctrine closely. Persevere in them, because if you do, you will save both yourself and your hearers."* (1 Tim. 4:16).

Thank You, Lord, for discernment to know true teaching to guide my family and me, as we follow Your truth with unwavering faithfulness.

- **Black represents darkness, death and mystery.** *"Blackest darkness is reserved for them"* (2 Pet. 2:17).

Thank You, Lord, that I do not have to fear black darkness because of Your love for me (Note: Rom. 8:38-39).

---

*It is not necessary to attach significance to the color of every object or article. However, there is significance in the colors that surround us. Colors take on significant meanings when you dream, or when you are visualizing some aspect of your faith, your future, or your family's well being. Being sensitive to color and what it represents can help you better focus on how to pray blessing on your home and family. The interpretation of the meanings of colors varies from author to author. These particular representations are based on the work of Ira Milligan (http://www.unlockingyourdreams.org/dream-dictionary/colors/).

You may have come across other interpretations of individual colors which are different. Allow the Lord to guide your thinking and prayers as to how to apply those interpretations.

COMPUTERS/MOBILE DEVICES/ INTERNET/DIGITAL MEDIA

Thank You, Lord, for the benefit of the digital age, for computers and the power of mobile devices. What helpful tools they are for education, relaxation, connecting with friends, and for work. I pray they will always be used only for good in my family and my life. I pray for our computers and those who will use them, for all our mobile devices and our use of *media*.

> *"I will be careful to live a blameless life— when will you come to help me? I will lead a life of integrity in my own home. I will refuse to look at anything vile and vulgar"* (Ps. 101:2-3 NLT).

Protect us from destructive, negative, or evil influences of Internet pornography, violent video games, or chat rooms. May You bless the activities we engage in through the internet and all other digital media. We ask for protection for our conscious and unconscious thoughts, wills, and emotions as we seek out various websites. Guard our hearts and minds (Note: Phil. 4:7), and as You said: *"… Lead us not into temptation, but deliver us from the evil one"* (Matt. 6:13). May every person who uses our computers and media find protection in You from the evil one.

Help us to use our time cautiously, not idly or wastefully. Instead, let us make the most of our time spent with communications technology and let it be treated as a gift from You.

- *"Don't lose your grip on love and loyalty. Tie them around your neck; carve their initials on your heart. Earn a reputation for living well in God's eyes and the eyes of the people"* (Prov. 3:3 MSG).
- *"I made a covenant with my eyes not to look lustfully at a young woman"* (Job 31:1).
- *"Turn my eyes away from worthless things; preserve my life according to your word"* (Ps. 119:37).
- *"We take captive every thought to make it obedient to Christ"* (2 Cor. 10:5).
- *"Whatever is true, whatever is noble, whatever is right, whatever is pure, whatever is lovely, whatever is admirable—if anything is excellent or praiseworthy—think about such things"* (Phil. 4:8).

> ❧ *"Acknowledge the God of your father, and serve him with wholehearted devotion and with a willing mind, for the Lord searches every heart and understands every desire and every thought"* (1 Chron. 28:9).

D

DOORS

Just as the Israelites put the blood of a lamb on their doorposts for supernatural protection (Note: Ex. 12:21-23), we plead the

blood of our Lamb, Jesus Christ, over these doorposts. We state here and now that this door is secure and will not open to the enemy.

As we walk in and out of this doorway many times every day, remind each person who passes through it that You *"have placed before you an open door that no one can shut. I know that you have little strength, yet you have kept my word and have not denied my name"* (Rev. 3:8). Lord, open doors of opportunity that You want my family and me to be involved with. Open doors that are best for us because

You planned them for our lives. I pray You will close doors that are not Your will for us right now, and give us wisdom and discernment to know the difference and to obey. Lead us in the right direction through every open door You place before us.

Lord, remind every person who walks through this door of Your words: *"tell you the truth, I am the door for the sheep"* (Jn. 10:7 NLT). Since You are that door, You have opened heaven to us, and we thank You. May we boldly, courageously, and in the power of Your Holy Spirit walk through every open door You place before us until You call us through the door into our eternal home with You.

DRAPERIES/WINDOW COVERINGS

Thank You, heavenly Father, for these draperies and window coverings, which admit light and hide the darkness. Thank You, Lord, that You are the Light of the world. (Note: Jn. 8:12). When we seek to know You better, and when You enter our lives, You open the curtains in our lives, and the darkness is overcome by light: *"The light shines in the darkness, and the darkness can never extinguish it"* (Jn. 1:5 NLT). You, Lord, are the Light of the world, and You say, Jesus spoke to the people once more and said, *"I am the light of the world. If you follow* me, you won't have to walk in darkness, because you will have the light that leads to life" (Jn. 8:12 NLT).

Thank You for being my family's *Light*.

Help us to see situations clearly, not through our own limited perspective but instead through Your eyes—the eyes of Jesus. Let us not be blinded by lies but instead stand firm with the belt of truth buckled around our waist (Note: Eph. 6:14), girding us up so that we might see this world as You see it.

E

EAGLES

Thank You, Lord, for Your magnificent promise, *"but those who hope in the Lord will renew their strength. They will soar on wings like eagles; they will run and not grow weary, they will walk and not be faint"* (Isa. 40:31).

I pray that every person who sees this eagle will think of You and the great value of knowing You, depending on You, and placing their hope in You. Bless every person who sees this eagle by reminding them that they can soar on wings like eagles as they trust in You.

Lord, eagles fly with such freedom while riding the winds, I pray my family will soar to new heights, enjoying the freedom of a relationship with You and freedom from all bondage. Your Word says, *"So if the Son sets you free, you will be free indeed"* (Jn. 8:36). I pray especially for __(name someone in your family, extended family, or a friend who is struggling right now).__ I pray that __(name the person)__ will experience freedom from their trials in Your perfect timing.

- *"The troubles of my heart have multiplied; free me from my anguish"* (Ps. 25:17).

Reveal through Your Holy Spirit any areas from past hurts or sins that need to be healed in order for us to receive complete and total freedom. May the freedom with which eagles fly encourage us to enjoy freedom from bondage and the freedom to be who You made us to *be*.

- *"You yourselves have seen what I did to Egypt, and how I carried you on eagles' wings and brought you to myself"* (Ex. 19:4).
- *"Who satisfies your desires with good things so that your youth is renewed like the eagle's"* (Ps. 103:5).

EXERCISE EQUIPMENT

Lord, I thank You for this exercise equipment. I pray for safety as we use it that it will be a source of strength and relaxation for my family and me. Let us not get drawn into vanity but instead remember to please You with our lives because, *"People look at the outward appearance, but the Lord looks at the heart"* (1 Sam. 16:7). Let us honor You with our bodies.

> *"Do you not know that your body is a temple of the Holy Spirit, who is in you, whom you have received from God? You are not your own; you were bought at a price. Therefore honor God with your body"* (1 Cor. 6:19-20).

God our Strength, I pray we will remember, as we strengthen our bodies, that You want us to be strong in the Lord and in his mighty power (Note: Eph. 6:10).

> *"For physical training is of some value, but godliness has value for all things, holding promise for both the present life and the life to come"* (1 Tim. 4:8).

Remind us as we grow stronger physically to put the priority in our lives on growing spiritually strong and fit as well; as You have said, *"Love the Lord your God with all your heart and with all your soul and with all your mind and with all your strength"* (Mk. 12:30).

FAMILY PHOTOS/FAMILY HERITAGE

(Future Generations, Past Generations)

Lord, as I see the family photographs on our wall, I pray for salvation and a relationship with You for each family member. Fill us with Your love, grace, and Holy Spirit. Please cover my family and extended family with the blood of Jesus for protection (Note: Rev. 1:5). I pray we will honor You, making you the center of our family. I pray that every person in our immediate family  and our extended family will love You. May we have godly relationships as we follow the commandments in Your Word (Note: 1 Thess. 5:11). May Your promise be true in our family:

> *"'As for me, this is my covenant with them,' says the Lord. 'My Spirit, who is on you, and my words that I have put in your mouth will not depart from your mouth, or from the mouths of your children, or from the mouths of their descendants from this time on and forever,' says the Lord"* (Isa. 59:21).

Grant this covenant for my family and extended family. I pray for specific family traits to continue—prayer, generosity, love, gracious words, and hard work, to name a few—and for You to tear down destructive traits—gossip, harshness, lack of respect, rebellion, deceit, addictions, control, manipulation, fear, or others. I ask You to bring to mind specific Scriptures You want me to pray for each person. Lead me to specific verses in the Bible I can pray in the future as these situations and family dynamics change.

Where unhealthy walls have been raised, please break them down. I pray for a spirit of unity, cooperation, reconciliation, patience, tolerance, acceptance, love, grace, and treating one another the way that we want to be treated (Note: Matt. 7:12). Help us support and encourage one another and go to battle for each other when necessary. Give us a new heart like You promise, *"And I will give you a new heart, and I will put a new spirit in you. I will take out your stony, stubborn heart and give you a tender, responsive heart. And I will put my Spirit in you so that you will follow my decrees and be careful to obey my regulations"* (Ezek. 36:26 NLT). Lord, continually give my family new, obedient hearts that fervently seek You.

May Your Spirit work in our lives so there is undeniable and unmistakable evidence of Your presence through Your Spirit living in us. Your Word says: *"The Spirit himself testifies with* our spirit that we are God's children. Now if we are children, then we are heirs—heirs of God and co-heirs with Christ" (Rom. 8:16-17).

Thank You for the Spirit who bears witness with our spirit that You are our heavenly *Father*.

- "*You are members of God's family*" (Eph. 2:19).
- "*He chose to give us birth through the word of truth, that we might be a kind of firstfruits of all he created*" (James 1:18).
- "*Listen, my son, to your father's instruction, and do not forsake your mother's teaching. They will be a garland to grace your head and a chain to adorn your neck*" (Prov. 1:8,9).
- "*Direct your children onto the right path, and when they are older, they will not leave it*" (Prov. 22:6 NLT).

FANS

Heavenly Father, thank You for this fan and the way it cools this room. As it provides us comfort, remind us that You are the God of all comfort (Note: 2 Cor. 1:3). I pray that as my family and I see this fan, You will remind us to "*fan into flame the gift of God, which is in you*" (2 Tim. 1:6).

Bless this fan to be a constant reminder of how we need to fan the flames of the gifts You have given us to be an encouragement to others so they can see You in us.

- *"Every good and perfect gift is from above, coming down from the Father of the heavenly lights, who does not change like shifting shadows"* (Jas. 1:17).

FARMS

As I look at this farm and the many paths around the house, barn, and fields, I am reminded that You love to lead my family and me along Your paths.

- *"Teach me your way, O Lord; lead me in a straight path"* (Ps. 27:11).

You have promised: *"Trust in the Lord with all your heart and lean not on your own understanding; in all your ways acknowledge him, and he will make your paths straight"* (Prov. 3:5-6). Thank You for leading us in Your ways, and I pray that every time anyone looks at this farm it will remind them of the way You lead our lives.

- *"He lets me rest in green meadows; he leads me beside peaceful streams"* (Ps. 23:2).

- *"He guards the paths of the just and protects those who are faithful to him"* (Prov. 2:8 NLT).

Thank You, Lord, for this promise: *"He will also send you rain for the seed you sow in the ground, and the food that comes from the land will be rich and plentiful. In that day your cattle will graze in broad meadows"* (Isa. 30:23). Your Word says:

- *"You care for the land and water it; you enrich it abundantly. The streams of God are filled with water to provide the people with grain, for so you have ordained it. You drench its furrows and level its ridges; you soften it with showers and bless its crops. You crown the year with your bounty, and your carts overflow with abundance. The grasslands of the desert overflow; the hills are clothed with gladness. The meadows are covered with flocks and the valleys are mantled with grain; they shout for joy and sing"* (Ps. 65:9-13).

Because You provide for us, we can continue eating from your own grapevine and fig tree and drinking from your own well (Note: Isa. 36:16). Thank You, Lord, that You have promised always to provide food and crops for us. Lord, I pray that as we look at the food You give us through crops, and how You cause everything to grow from a seed, help us remember the principle of sowing and reaping.

- *"Now he who supplies seed to the sower and bread for food will also supply and increase your store of seed and will enlarge the harvest of your righteousness"* (2 Cor. 9:10).

Thank You that You love to multiply the good in our lives many times over. Lord, remind us of the way You provide everything we need. Let our roots grow deep in You that we may produce good fruit. May Your purposes be accomplished in my family, extended family, friends, and in my own life.

- *"In him we were also chosen, having been predestined according to the plan of him who works out everything in conformity with the purpose of his will"* (Eph. 1:11).

Lord, as we look upon the wells on this farm, remind us that You are the Wellspring of *Life*.

- *"Isaac reopened the wells that had been dug in the time of his father Abraham, which the Philistines had stopped up after Abraham died, and he gave them the same names his father had given them"* (Gen. 26:18).

- *"With joy you will draw water from the wells of salvation"* (Isa. 12:3).

- *"Above all else, guard your heart, for it is the wellspring of life"* (Prov. 4:23).

- *"The well where God said to Moses, 'Gather the people together and I will give them water'"* (Num. 21:16-17).

- *"Whoever believes in me, as the Scripture has said, streams of living water will flow from him"* (Jn. 7:38).

And Lord, as we watch the weathervane on this farm, may we remember You hold all weather and all seasons in Your hand.

- *"No one can escape the weather—it's there. And no one can escape from God"* (Job 37:2 MSG).

- *"Who do you suppose carves canyons for the downpours of rain, and charts the route of thunderstorms that bring water to unvisited fields, deserts no one ever lays eyes on, drenching the useless wastelands so they're carpeted with wildflowers and grass? And who do you think is the father of rain and dew, the mother of ice and frost? You don't for a minute imagine these marvels of weather just happen, do you?"* (Job 38:22-23 MSG).

- *"Friends love through all kinds of weather, and families stick together in all kinds of trouble"* (Prov. 17:17 MSG).

- *"As the rain and the snow come down from heaven, and do not return to it without watering the earth and making it bud and flourish, so that it yields seed for the sower and bread for the eater, so is my word that goes out from my mouth: It will not return to me empty, but will accomplish what I desire and achieve the purpose for which I sent it"* (Isa. 55:10-11).

- *"You care for the land and water it; you enrich it abundantly. The streams of God are filled with water to provide the people with grain, for so you have ordained it. You drench its furrows and level its ridges; you soften it with showers and bless its crops. You crown the year with you bounty, and your carts overflow with abundance. The grasslands of the desert overflow: the hills are clothed with gladness. The meadows are covered with flocks and the valleys are mantled with grain; they shout for joy and sing"* (Ps. 65:9-13).

FENCES/GATES

I pray that whoever enters through the fences and gates of our  lives will be healthy, wholesome influences and not people who will harm us or distract us from Your will and plan for our lives. Bless all that come in and keep harmful influences away. Show my children and me when to shut the gate to negative influences or negative influencers, and to have healthy boundaries in our lives. Thank You, Lord, that You are the great Shepherd of my family, who enters through the gates of our hearts (Note: Jn. 10:2).

Thank You, O Lord, that Your Word says that faith in You is like a gate. Your Word reminds us: *"For wide is the gate and broad is the road that leads to destruction, and many enter through it. But small is the gate and narrow the road that leads to life, and only a few find it"* (Matt. 7:13-14). May everyone who walks through this gate or sees this gate do so with thanksgiving in their hearts (Note: Ps. 100:4) and be reminded of the salvation You offer in Jesus. Let us choose the "narrow gate" which You have promised leads to eternal life.

You are an awesome Lord who made everything to praise *You*.

- *"Lift up your heads, O you gates; be lifted up, you ancient doors, that the King of glory may come in"* (Ps. 24:7).

We ask Your blessing on these fences and gates, just as fences are physical markers of our land or territory, let it remind my family, extended family, friends, and me as a physical reminder that You are the King of Glory, and that we must open the doors of our hearts so You may come in.

FIREPLACES

Just as a fire in a fireplace consumes the wood on the grate, send the fire of the Holy Spirit to consume my family and me with a love for You. You appeared to Abraham as a smoking firepot with a blazing torch (Note: Gen. 15:17). May every person who looks at this fire and enjoys its warmth, have eyes to see You, as Moses did.

- *"There the angel of the Lord appeared to him in flames of fire from within a bush. Moses saw that though the bush was on fire it did not burn up"* (Ex. 3:2).

- *"Ignite the hearts of my family to call on You, Lord, because fire is one way You describe Yourself in the Bible: 'for our God is a consuming fire'"* (Heb. 12:29).

Gracious Lord Jesus, thank You that You say, *"Is not my word like fire?"* (Jer. 23:29). Let Your Word be like fire in this household. I pray You will send Your Word to consume this household with a burning love for You and a love for others as naturally as we love ourselves (Note: Matt. 22:37-39). Burn away the impurities in our lives as we prepare for that time when we will see You face to face (Note: 1 Pet. 1:7).

FISH

Lord, as we see these fish we thank You for Your willingness to teach us as You did Your first followers: *"Jesus called out to them, 'Come, follow me, and I will show you how to fish for people.'"* (Matt. 4:19 NLT).

Lord, just as You fed more than 5,000 people with five loaves and two fish—a miracle—we thank You for providing food for us and for performing miracles even today. Remind us of that every time we look at fish. When we have fear or doubt that the Creator of the whole earth and everything in it can really provide for us, cause us to remember You are God and You do not lie (Note: Tit. 1:2). Lord, You perform miracles daily. Many times, we don't even see them.

Sometimes, Lord, things take longer to work out in our lives than we would like them to—but we know Your plan is the best (Note: Eph. 1:9). Teach us to remember that You are in charge of everything, including our food needs. Thank You that You even use fish to teach us of Your ways.

- *"Speak to the earth, and it will instruct you. Let the fish in the sea speak to you"* (Job 12:8).

FLAGS

Thank You, Lord, for our flag. This flag reminds me that You, Lord, are Jehovah Nissi ("NEE-see"), the Lord My Banner. As this flag flies to remind us of the price *paid* for our freedom, I thank You for the real, lasting freedom my family has in knowing You. We're so grateful for our freedom, but we thank You more for the freedom we have in Christ. Help us never to take it for granted, but to relish that freedom as a way to serve each other humbly in love (Note: Gal. 5:3). Thank You that

You use physical items like flags to remind Your people of Your power.

"Then the Lord said to Moses, Write this on a scroll as something to be remembered and make sure that Joshua hears it. Moses built an altar and called it The Lord is my Banner" (Ex. 17:14-15).

As we look upon the flag of our country or state, let it be a reminder to pray for those who are in a position of authority over us (Note: 1 Tim. 2:1-2). We pray You will give our leaders wisdom as they plan the future of our city, our state, and our country. Let us have a love for our homeland, but let us have an even greater love for You and Your kingdom.

FLOORS

Lord, I pray that as we walk across the floor, You will keep us from stumbling and bless our steps as we follow Your laws and

commands. I pray our every step will be worthy and pleasing to You as our Lord (Note: 1 Thess. 2:12).

You remind us, *"Therefore be careful how you walk, not as unwise men but as wise"* (Eph. 5:15 NASB), so bless the people who walk across this floor and anoint this floor so that we stay in step with Your Spirit (Note: Gal. 5:25). Thank You for the ability You gave to *"keep [us] from stumbling, and to make [us] stand in the presence of His glory blameless with great joy, to the only God our Savior, through Jesus Christ our Lord, be glory, majesty, dominion and authority, before all time and now and forever. Amen"* (Jude 24,25 NASB, brackets added).

I pray that if someone in my family's life is not in step with You, You will show them Your power and reorder their steps with Your Words in the Bible through Your Holy Spirit. *"Teach me how to live, O Lord. Lead me along the right path"* (Ps. 27:11 NLT).

May every step we take be based upon the firm foundation that You provide because You say, *"The Lord makes firm the steps of the one who delights in him"* (Ps. 37:23). May we experience Your blessing of walking as Jesus walked when He lived on this earth (Note: 1 Jn. 2:6). Anoint every person who walks across this floor, and use this floor to remind us of how You are guarding our every step.

> *"Listen, my son, accept what I say, and the years of your life will be many. I guide you in the way of wisdom and lead you along straight paths. When you walk, your steps will not be hampered; when you run, you will not stumble. Hold on to*

instruction, do not let it go; guard it well, for it is your life" (Prov. 4:10, 13).

- "Go, walk through the length and breadth of the land, for I am giving it to you" (Gen. 13:17).

- "I will walk among you and be your God, and you will be my people" (Lev. 26:12).

- "Walk in obedience to all that the Lord your God has commanded you, so that you may live and prosper and prolong your days in the land that you will possess" (Deut. 5:33).

- "That I may walk before the Lord in the land of the living" (Ps. 116:9).

- "The Lord makes firm the steps of the one who delights in him; though he may stumble, he will not fall, for the Lord upholds him with his hand" (Ps. 37:23-24).

FLOWERS

Lord, as my family looks at flowers, remind each of us of Your desire for us to be a fragrance of Christ, reflecting His beautiful traits.

- "Now he uses us to spread the knowledge of Christ everywhere, like a sweet perfume. Our lives are a Christ-like fragrance rising up to God ... to those who are being saved, we are a life-giving perfume" (Cor. 2:14-16 NLT).

- *"Live a life filled with love, following the example of Christ. He loved us and offered himself as a sacrifice for us, a pleasing aroma to God"* (Eph. 5:2 NLT).

Thank You, Lord, for the beauty of flowers. You are the Creator of beauty and *"every good and perfect gift [including the beauty of nature all around us] comes from above, coming down from the Father of lights, with whom there is no variation or shifting shadow"* (Jas. 1:17, brackets added). We love how creative You are, how diverse Your creation is, and how much of Your genius is on display every day throughout Your creation (Note: Rom. 1:19-21).

Thank You that these flowers remind us how special and unique we are in Your eyes. Their very existence is a form of poetry to us—as You wrote in Your own book of poetry, *"Like a lily among thorns is my darling among the young women"* (Song. 2:2). Help us to acknowledge our own intrinsic beauty and uniqueness.

- *"And why do you worry about clothes? See how the lilies of the field grow. They do not labor or spin. Yet I tell you that not even Solomon in all his splendor was dressed like one of these. If that is how God clothes the grass of the field, which is here today and tomorrow is thrown into the fire, will he not much more clothe you, O you of little faith?"* (Matt. 6:28-30).

FOOD

Lord, food reminds me You are the vine and we are the branches; we receive nutrition from You. We can enjoy life because of You and what You give us. Thank You for

feeding us spiritually, physically, emotionally, relationally, and mentally each day (Note: Jn. 15:1-7). Your promise to us is, *"If you remain in me and my words remain in you, ask whatever you wish, and it will be given you"* (Jn. 15:7). May this food remind us that You are our source of life, joy, peace, and help. I pray we will digest Your Word, the Bible, as often as we eat our physical food, so we can enjoy the best of life. Your Word says, *"When your words showed up, I ate them—swallowed them whole. What a feast! What delight I took in being yours, O God, God-of-the-Angel-Armies!"* (Jer. 15:16 MSG).

Thank You, Lord, that You are a giving God who has always provided for Your people, *"He sent them all the food they could eat"* (Ps. 78:25). Your promise is to supply all of our needs (Note: Phil. 4:19). Lord, give us Your long-term, eternal perspective on life.

- *"Do not work for food that spoils, but for food that endures to eternal life, which the Son of Man will give you. On him God the Father has placed his seal of approval"* (Jn. 6:27).

- *"From the fruit of his mouth a man's stomach is filled; with the harvest from his lips he is satisfied"* (Prov. 18:20).

- *"Give us today the food we need"* (Matt. 6:11 NLT).

- *"John replied, 'If you have two shirts, give one to the poor. If you have food, share it with those who are hungry'"* (Lk. 3:11 NLT).

- *"You satisfy my soul with the richest foods. My mouth will sing [your] praise with joyful lips"* (Ps. 63:5 GW).

FOOTSTOOLS

Thank You, Lord, that no thought I have of You can compare to how awesome You really are. You remind me, *"Let us go to the sanctuary of the Lord; let us worship at the footstool of his throne"* (Ps. 132:7 NLT). Please strengthen my desire to obey You more and listen for Your commands by sitting at Your footstool. Thank You that I can read the Bible and that You love

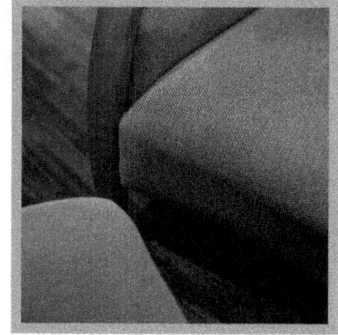

to teach me. Nothing in heaven or earth can compare to You because You are beyond any thought I can have.

> *"This is what the Lord says: 'Heaven is my throne, and the earth is my footstool'"* (Isa. 66:1).

May we be reminded every time we see this footstool that You love to teach us individually as we sit at Your feet, even though You are beyond our total comprehension. Thank You that You say, *"For my thoughts are not your thoughts, neither are your ways my ways"* (Isa. 55:8).

FRUIT

Heavenly Father, Creator of all things, thank You for fruit. Not only did You give it to us for physical nourishment, but also for a spiritual symbol. One of Your first commands was to eat fruit (Note: Gen. 2:16), and as Christians we are to distinguish between true and false prophets by the fruit they bear (Note: Matt. 7:15-20). As we look at and eat this fruit, may it stand as a reminder to us that we are to bear good fruit in our own lives, as a result of our communion with You. Bless everyone who partakes of this fruit, in Your name.

- *"But the fruit of the Spirit is love, joy, peace, forbearance, kindness, goodness, faithfulness, gentleness and self-control. Against such things there is no law"* (Gal. 5:22-23).

- *"The land produced vegetation: plants bearing seed according to their kinds and trees bearing fruit with seed in it according to their kinds. And God saw that it was good"* (Gen. 1:12).

- *"The tongue has the power of life and death, and those who love it will eat its fruit"* (Prov. 18:21).

- *"I am the vine; you are the branches. If you remain in me and I in you, you will bear much fruit; apart from me you can do nothing"* (John 15:5).

G

GLASS/GLASSES/CUPS

Thank You, heavenly Father, for these glasses. Thank You for Your promise of the time when You will come back to earth and set up Your heavenly kingdom.

- *"The wall was made of jasper, and the city of pure gold, as pure as glass. The foundations of the city walls were decorated with every kind of precious stone ... The great street of the city was of pure gold, like transparent glass"* (Rev. 21:18, 19, 21).

Bless this glass to remind us of Your greatness, Your power, and the glory of Your future kingdom. May each person who sees these attributes reflect on whether or not they have a relationship with You and be in that City that has transparent glass for walls.

Let these glasses also stand in our lives as a symbol of the purity You desire for us. Let us not become cracked or dirtied by the world but rather *"Come out from them and be separate"* (2 Cor. 6:17). Let us remember to interact with the world without conforming to it (Note: Rom. 12:2), and let us stand in this world as pure and shining as glass.

> *"One day he and his disciples got in a boat. 'Let's cross the lake,' he said. And off they went. It was smooth sailing, and he fell asleep. A terrific storm came up suddenly on the lake. Water poured in, and they were about to capsize. They woke Jesus: 'Master, Master, we're going to drown!' Getting to his feet, he told the wind, 'Silence!' and the waves, 'Quiet down!' They did it. The lake became smooth as glass"* (Lk. 8:22-24, MSG).

- *"You prepare a table before me in the presence of my enemies. You anoint my head with oil; my cup overflows"* (Ps. 23:5).

- *"Then [Jesus] took a cup, and when he had given thanks, he gave it to them, saying, 'Drink from it, all of you. This is my blood of the covenant, which is poured out for many for the forgiveness of sins. I tell you, I will not drink from this fruit of the vine from now on until that day when I drink it new with you in my Father's kingdom'"* (Matt. 26:27-29).

GLOBE/MAPS

Note: You can pray for your world, country, or neighborhood using a globe or a map. As you pray, touch the geographic place on the globe or map as a reminder of the area for which you are praying. A picture of the area or of people in the area can be present as you pray while pointing to the specific area or issues you are praying for.

Lord, I thank You that You hold the world in Your hands. Everyone and everything You created is under Your control because You say, *"through whom He made the worlds, ages and all that is in them"* (Heb. 1:3).

- *"The earth is the Lord's, and everything in it. The world and all its people belong to him"* (Ps. 24:1 NLT).

As I look at this map, I pray *for:*

THE WORLD

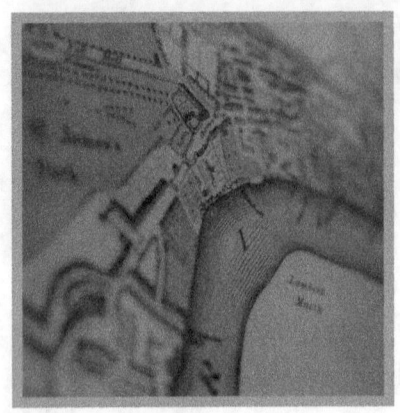

Pray for a challenge in the world that is touching your heart like disease, hunger, AIDS, lack of clean water, the orphan crisis, the persecuted church ... the list goes on. Pray against destructive weather phenomena, or for places where the destruction is caused by war. Pray that the gospel be heard the world over, that God would send those who can carry His good news to every nation, tribe, and tongue. Did someone else put the world in his care? Who set the whole world in place? (Note: Job 34:13 NLT).

COUNTRIES

Pray for specific countries, their leaders, any cultural unrest or physical problems they may be encountering (famine, drought, civil war, financial upheaval, etc.), and any needs God leads you to pray for in a special way.

◈ *"I will certainly bring my people back again from all the countries where I will scatter them in my fury. I will bring them back to this very city and let them live in peace and safety"* (Jer. 32:37 NLT).

ISRAEL

Lord we pray for the peace of Jerusalem and Israel because God says: I will bless those who bless you, and whoever curses you I will curse; and all peoples on earth will be blessed through you. (Note: Gen. 12:3)

God's Word tells us, pray for the peace of Jerusalem: *"May those who love you be secure. May there be peace within your walls and security within your citadels"* (Ps. 122:6-7). The United States has traditionally been an ally of Israel, and as a result, God has blessed our country in direct response to His Word written above. Pray that our government will continue to support the nation of Israel, thus continuing to invite God's blessing and protection on our nation.

UNITED STATES

Pray for our president, senators, representatives, armed forces, judges and justice departments, state and local representatives and all staff, affiliated, and unaffiliated parties. God wants us to pray regularly for our leaders.

> *"I urge you, first of all, to pray for all people. Ask God to help them; intercede on their behalf, and give thanks for them. Pray this way for kings and all who are in authority so that we can live peaceful and quiet lives marked by godliness and dignity. This is good and pleases God our Savior"* (1 Tim. 2:1-3 NLT).

Pray for the following areas for your country, state, city: arts/entertainment, business, education, family, government and unaffiliated parties.

STATES

Begin by praying for your own state first, and then the states surrounding you—especially remembering those where extended family live. When you pray for your state, pray for the elected officials, for the needs in the area, for enough food for all the people, a reduction in crime, an increase in justice, jobs, peace, and especially for the Lord's righteous rule to reign over your state.

Pray for a cleansing of the land, people and companies, and ask the Lord to bless the state and its inhabitants in all geographic, physical, spiritual, and economic areas.

CITIES

Pray for the city where you live and for specific cities that touch your heart or for challenges in the news taking place in specific cities. For example, pray for your city, the elected officials, the schools, churches in your area, hungry children, abused or neglected children and families, and other specific needs. Be sure to pray for arts/entertainment (including sports, business, education, textbooks), families (physical and spiritual), government (and laws), media (internet), and religion (all churches).

LOCAL AREAS

Pray for areas around your home, in your neighborhood, where your children go to school, other schools, the schoolteachers and boards, office buildings, apartments, or other activities on your mind and heart.

HOUSE

Pray God's blessing on the people in your house, your apartment complex, yard, farm, condo, or wherever you call home. Also, pray for the foundation and work your way up to the roof. (Note: Read chapter four, *Your Property and Its Surroundings*.)

ROOMS

Pray for the rooms of your home and special requests for the people you feel are in need and tugging on your heart. God put that concern on your heart, and He is nudging you to pray. (See chapters five through eight.)

PEOPLE

You can turn to a specific room in this guidebook for prayer and use one of the prayers there as a model to guide you in praying for specific family and friends. For example, if a friend is struggling in their marriage, use the prayers in the family room or master bedroom as a template or as starters for your own prayers. If a child in your family or a friend's child is facing a difficult season in life, you can use the children's room prayers as guides for praying for a specific area.

GRASS

Thank You, Lord, for Your guidance in our lives through Your Word. As I see the grass planted here, I am reminded of Your promise, *"The grass withers and the flowers fade beneath the breath of the Lord. And so it is with people. The grass withers and the flowers fade, but the word of our God stands forever"* (Isa. 40:7-8 NLT).

As I look at the beautiful green grass, I want to thank You that You use grass in Your Word as a reminder of how short life really is but how long Your love lasts:

- *"As for man, his days are like grass, he flourishes like a flower of the field; the wind blows over it and it is gone, and its place remembers it no more. But from everlasting to everlasting the Lord's love is with those who fear him, and his righteousness with their children's children— with those who keep his covenant and remember to obey his precepts"* (Ps. 103:15-18).

H

HORSES

Thank You for all the animals on farms and ranches, but thank You especially for the horses. They remind me of Your promise to lead me like I lead the horse. Guide us along the best path for our lives, and let us be responsive to Your every direction for us, following You closely.

- *"The Lord says, 'I will guide you along the best pathway for your life. I will advise you and watch over you. Do not be like a senseless horse or mule that needs a bit and bridle to keep it under control." Many sorrows come to the wicked, but unfailing love surrounds those who trust the Lord'"* (Ps. 32:8-10 NLT).

- *"When you go out to battle against your enemies, and see horses and chariots and people more numerous than you, do not be afraid of them; for the Lord your God is with you, who brought you up from the land of Egypt"* (Deut. 20:1 NKJV).

- *"The horse is prepared for the day of battle, but deliverance is of the Lord"* (Prov. 21:31 NKJV).

K

KEYS

Thank You, Lord, that Your Word says, *"I will give you the keys of the kingdom of heaven; whatever you bind on earth will be bound in heaven, and whatever you loose on earth will be loosed in heaven"* (Matt. 16:19). Thank You that the keys You have given every believer are the authority, the privilege, and the access to Your power and grace through the Holy Spirit. We are now a part of Your priesthood (Note: 1 Pet. 2:9). Let me use the key of prayer by the power of Your Holy Spirit, in the strong name of Jesus, to release Your will and Word into our family and home.

Lord, You know I sometimes misplace my keys. I pray especially that I will never lose sight of the prayer keys or the keys of the kingdom You have given me. I pray that when it seems like we are locked out of knowing Your will, You will remind me of Your promise.

> *"See, I have placed before you an open door that no one can shut. I know that you have little strength, yet you have kept my word and have not denied my name"* (Rev. 3:8)

Help me to allow You to rule in my life, which Your promises say will give me the desires of my heart (Note: Ps. 37:4). Each time I see my keys, remind me of the power through prayer You have given me. May I use my spiritual keys to open the open door to Your will for my life.

L

LAMPS/LIGHTS

Lord, as I pray for the lamps and overhead lights right now, I am reminded of what You said: *"My light will shine for you just a little longer. Walk in the light while you can, so the darkness will not overtake you. Those who walk in the darkness cannot see where they are going"* (Jn. 12:35 NLT). I pray my family will live their lives in accordance with Your Word and Your light because *"Your Word is a lamp for my feet and a light for my path"* (Ps. 119:105). May Your truth in the Scriptures shine brightly, providing light which causes all darkness or evil to flee this room and every room of my home. Thank You that You are the Father of lights (Note: James 1:17). Thank You for leading me in Your light.

- *"By day the Lord went ahead of them in a pillar of cloud to guide them on their way and by night in a pillar of fire to give them light, so that they could travel by day or night"* (Ex. 13:21).

- *"You, Lord, are my lamp; the Lord turns my darkness into light"* (2 Sam. 22:29).

- *"The people who walk in darkness will see a great light; those who live in a dark land, the light will shine on them"* (Isa. 9:2 NASB).

- *"In the same way, let your light shine before others, that they may see your good deeds and glorify your Father in heaven"* (Matt. 5:16).

- *"You are all children of the light and children of the day. We do not belong to the night or to the darkness"* (1 Thess. 5:5).

- *"You are the light of the world. A city on a hill cannot be hidden. Neither do people light a lamp and put it under a bowl. Instead they put it on its stand, and it gives light to everyone in the house. In the same way, let your light shine before men, that they may see your good deeds and praise your Father in heaven"* (Matt. 5:14-16).

- *"You light a lamp for me. The Lord, my God, lights up my darkness"* (Ps. 18:28 NLT).

- *"The teaching of your word gives light, so even the simple can understand"* (Ps. 119:130).

LAND

Lord, I ask you to cleanse this land from past offenses, I repent and ask for forgiveness on behalf of the people who allowed the sin. I ask you cover it with the blood of Jesus and call forth all the God ordained blessings for this land. (Note: read pgs. 31-36 for instructions to pray over your land.)

- *"Therefore God exalted him to the highest place and gave him the name that is above every name, that at the name of Jesus every knee should bow, in heaven and on earth and under the earth, and every tongue acknowledge that Jesus Christ is Lord, to the glory of God the Father"* (Phil. 2:9-11).

- *"I have given you authority to trample on snakes and scorpions and to overcome all the power of the enemy; nothing will harm you"* (Lk. 10:19).

> ໖ "If my people, who are called by my name, will humble themselves and pray and seek my face and turn from their wicked ways, then I will hear from heaven, and I will forgive their sin and will heal their land" (2 Chron. 7:14).

LIONS

This picture of a lion reminds me that You are the all-powerful King of the universe. It reminds me that You have promised  in Scripture to always provide for me and my family: *"Taste and see that the Lord is good. Oh, the joys of those who take refuge in him! Fear the Lord, you his godly people, for those who fear him will have all they need. Even strong young lions sometimes go hungry, but those who trust in the Lord will lack no good thing"* (Ps. 34:8-10 NLT).

If any member of my family is facing a difficult time, I pray You will remind them that You will always provide what is best. Even though lions may lack, my family will not. We can count on You to give us everything we need daily.

Thank You, Lord, that You are able to shut the mouths of the lions—those harmful situations in our lives—as You did for Daniel.

- *"My God sent his angel, and he shut the mouths of the lions. They have not hurt me, because I was found innocent in his sight. Nor have I ever done any wrong before you, O king"* (Dan. 6:22).

May You protect us from potentially harmful circumstances, and may we remember to give You the glory by giving You the credit for our protection. Thank You that You are the mighty Lion of Judah.

- *"Then one of the elders said to me, 'Do not weep! See, the Lion of the tribe of Judah, the Root of David, has triumphed. He is able to open the scroll and its seven seals'"* (Rev. 5:5).

LOCKS/PROTECTION

Thank You, Lord, for the locks and security system on the doors and windows. Even though we have locks, latches and alarms for our security, we know that You alone are our true protection and security.

- *"My help comes from the Lord, the Maker of heaven and earth. He will not let your foot slip—he who watches over* you will not slumber; bless us with the security of Your love" (Ps. 121:2-3 NIV).

- "I say to the Lord, 'You are my God.' Hear, Lord, my cry for mercy. Sovereign Lord, my strong deliverer, you shield my head in the day of battle" (Ps. 140:6-7 NIV).

- "Anoint our doors and locks with Your secure, loving presence, and may Your guardian angels protect us constantly" (Heb. 1:7).

- "For I am convinced that neither death nor life, neither angels nor demons, neither the present nor the future, nor any powers, neither height nor depth, nor anything else in all creation, will be able to separate us from the love of God that is in Christ Jesus our Lord" (Rom. 8:38-39).

Pray Psalm 91 for protection:

Those who live in the shelter of the Most High will find rest in the shadow of the Almighty. This I declare about the Lord: He alone is my refuge, my place of safety; he is my God, and I trust him.

For He will rescue you from every trap and protect you from deadly disease. He will cover you with his feathers. He will shelter you with his wings. His faithful promises are your armor and protection.

Do not be afraid of the terrors of the night, nor the arrow that flies in the day. Do not dread the disease that stalks in darkness, nor the disaster that strikes at midday.

Though a thousand fall at your side, though ten thousand are dying around you, these evils will not touch you. Just open your eyes, and see how the wicked are punished.

If you make the Lord your refuge, if you make the Most High your shelter, no evil will conquer you; no plague will come near your home.

For he will order his angels to protect you wherever you go. They will hold you up with their hands so you won't even hurt your foot on a stone. You will trample upon lions and cobras; you will crush fierce lions and serpents under your feet!

The Lord says, "I will rescue those who love me. I will protect those who trust in my name. When they call on me, I will answer; I will be with them in trouble. I will rescue and honor them. I will reward them with a long life and give them my salvation."

PS. 91, NLT

M

MIRRORS

El Roi, You are the *"God Who Sees"* (Gen. 16:13). Please help me to see my reflection, the way You view me. You are perfect and You make no mistakes. Enable me to look in the mirror and see the beautiful child You lovingly created. Please turn off the voices in the back of my mind that criticize and frown on every wrinkle or imperfection. Guard my heart from the media fallacy of a perfect outer image. I look the way You want me to look. I have the skin tone, the facial features, and body type You desire me to have because You *"knit me together in my mother's womb"* (Ps. 139:13). I hear Your voice telling me that *"I am fearfully and wonderfully made"* (Ps. 139:14).

Lord, I know the only way I can see in a mirror is when light is present. In the same way, I see in the mirror of the Bible when You, my Light, are present. I know that in You no darkness dwells. You enlighten every man (Note: Jn. 1:9). I come to You knowing that darkness must flee in the presence of Your Light. I embrace You, O Lord, as my Light in every corner of my life.

Your Word is a mirror for my soul, O Lord. I know there is a dangerous possibility that I will read the Scriptures, close the book and refuse to act on what I have read. This is like looking at my reflection in a mirror, then forgetting how I look (Note: Jas. 1:23). So Lord, may I not be a hearer or reader only, but a doer of Your Word. Grant me, Holy Spirit, by Your mercy, the ability to follow through in what I read and to put Your Word to action into my life.

Lord, I know I will never fully comprehend You and Your ways, even as I read Your Word because You've said: *"Now we see things imperfectly as in a cloudy mirror, but then we will see everything with perfect clarity. All that I know now is partial and incomplete, but then I will know everything completely, just as God now knows me completely"* (1 Cor. 13:12 NLT). Yet, even in my partial and incomplete sight, let me have eyes to see and ears to hear all that You have for me today.

Lord, help us to see ourselves through Your eyes—eyes of affirmation, with no condemnation (Note: Rom. 8:1). Reveal to us what faults need to be corrected, and give us the courage to change. We ask that You continue to reveal wounds in our souls until we are set free.

- *"I will pour out my Spirit on all people. Your sons and daughters will prophesy, your old men will dream dreams, your young men will see visions"* (Joel 2:28).

- *"When they arrived, Samuel saw Eliab and thought, 'Surely the Lord's anointed stands here before the Lord.' But the Lord said to Samuel, 'Do not consider his appearance or his height, for I have rejected him. The Lord does not look at the things people look at. People look at the outward appearance, but the Lord looks at the heart'"* (1 Sam. 16:6-7).

- *"Your eyes saw my unformed body; all the days ordained for me were written in your book before one of them came to be.*

How precious to me are your thoughts, God! How vast is the sum of them! Were I to count them, they would outnumber the grains of sand—when I awake, I am still with you" (Ps. 139:16-18).

- "I know the plans that I have for you, declares the Lord. They are plans for peace and not disaster, plans to give you a future filled with hope" (Jer. 29:11 GW).

- "The Lord directs the steps of the godly. He delights in every detail of their lives" (Ps. 37:23 NLT).

- "And I am certain that God, who began the good work within you, will continue his work until it is finally finished on the day when Christ Jesus returns" (Phil. 1:6 NLT).

- "I took you from the ends of the earth, from its farthest corners I called you. I said, "You are my servant"; I have chosen you and have not rejected you. So do not fear, for I am with you; do not be dismayed, for I am your God. I will strengthen you and help you; I will uphold you with my righteous right hand" (Isa. 41:9,10).

- "For the Lord your God is living among you. He is a mighty savior. He will take delight in you with gladness. With his love, he will calm all your fears. He will rejoice over you with joyful songs" (Zeph. 3:17 NLT).

MUSIC/MUSICAL INSTRUMENTS

Thank You, Lord, that we can play music to honor and praise You. Thank You for the variety of instruments available to us and how each one adds to the overall symphony of sound that pleases You. We offer each one up to You to glorify You at all times.

Lord, we know the power of worship and praise, and we seek to make music and to sing a new song to You (Note: Ps. 96:1; Isa. 42:10). When we worship You through the music You created, barriers are broken and intimacy is established. We pray that these musical instruments will always be used in worship of You and solely for Your purposes, whether to create an intimate moment of supplication with just You or through a concert for many.

Thank You for the story in Your Word about the music of David and how it drove away an evil spirit that was tormenting King Saul (Note: 1 Sam. 16:14-23). Music is a gift from You that feeds our souls and causes the devil to flee. Gracious heavenly Father, thank You that we can sing, and enjoy what we are singing. We praise You because You tell us, *"Worship the Lord with gladness; come before him with joyful songs"* (Ps. 100:2).

- *"Let everything that has breath praise the Lord. Praise the Lord"* (Ps. 150:6).

Help us all, family and friends, to make a joyful noise of praise, regardless of how well we think we sing (Note: Ps. 105:43). Let the words of our songs and the melodies of our hearts be both consistent with Your will and an encouragement to others. You love to fill our hearts with Your Holy Spirit so that we sing *"to one another with psalms and hymns and spiritual songs"* (Eph. 5:19).

Lord Jesus, when You walked on this earth, You sang praises just before the cross (Note: Mk. 14:26). So I pray that we will love You and use our voices to praise You, encourage others, and encourage ourselves.

- *"Is any one of you in trouble? He should pray. Is anyone happy? Let him sing songs of praise"* (Jas. 5:13).

May our singing be used to bring joy and glory to You.

- *"David and all the people of Israel were celebrating before the Lord, singing songs and playing all kinds of musical instruments—lyres, harps, tambourines, castanets, and cymbals"* (2 Sam. 6:5 NLT).

- *"Praise him with the sounding of the trumpet, praise him with the harp and lyre, praise him with tambourine and dancing, praise him with the strings and flute, praise him with the clash of cymbals, praise him with resounding cymbals. Let everything that has breath praise the Lord. Praise the Lord"* (Ps. 150:3-6).

- *"All these men were under the direction of their fathers as they made music at the house of the Lord. Their responsibilities included the playing of cymbals, harps, and lyres at the house of God"* (1 Chron. 25:6 NLT).

- *"They marched into Jerusalem to the music of harps, lyres, and trumpets, and they proceeded to the Temple of the Lord"* (2 Chron. 20:28 NLT).

- *"Praise the Lord with melodies on the lyre; make music for him on the ten-stringed harp"* (Ps. 33:2 NLT).

- *"Let the message of Christ dwell among you richly as you teach and admonish one another with all wisdom through psalms, hymns, and songs from the Spirit, singing to God with gratitude in your hearts"* (Col. 3:16).

- *"He put a new song in my mouth, a hymn of praise to our God. Many will see and fear the Lord and put their trust in him"* (Ps. 40:3).

N

NATURE SCENES

Lord God, Creator of all, You have a keen appreciation for order, beauty, and creativity. You tell us: *"For ever since the world was created, people have seen the earth and sky. Through everything God made, they can clearly see His invisible qualities—His eternal *power and divine nature. So they have no excuse for not knowing God"* (Rom. 1:20 NLT).

I pray that the truth of who You are, the Creator of the universe, will lead each one seeing this picture to desire a closer

relationship with You. Help us to connect with You through nature, appreciate its beauty, and realize that we are really appreciating You. Thank You, Lord, for giving us seasons and cycles in the weather, evidence that You are alive and involved in every aspect of our lives (Note: Gen. 8:22). Thank You that Your Word promises every season will change which gives me great hope when there is a challenging season in my family or in my life.

Thank You, Lord, for the variety of trees You have *made.*

- *"I will plant trees in the barren desert—cedar, acacia, myrtle, olive, cypress, fir, and pine"* (Isa. 41:19 NLT). You are such a creative heavenly Father!

- *"God spoke: 'Earth, green up! Grow all varieties of seed-bearing plants, every sort of fruit-bearing tree.' And there it was. Earth produced green seed-bearing plants, all varieties,* and fruit-bearing trees of all sorts. God saw that it was good" (Gen. 1:11 MSG).

- "I will send you rain in its season, and the ground will yield its crops and the trees their fruit" (Lev. 26:4).

- "Yet he has not left himself without testimony: He has shown kindness by giving you rain from heaven and crops in their seasons; he provides you with plenty of food and fills your hearts with joy" (Acts 14:17).

NEEDLEPOINT/TAPESTRIES

Thank You for the ways in which You remind us of how You work in our lives through items like this tapestry. While the underside of this beautiful tapestry looks like a mess, it is a wonderful reflection of what You do with everything in our lives.

- "And we know that God causes everything to work together for the good of those who love God and are called according to his purpose for them" (Rom. 8:28 NLT).

As I have heard it said before, my first two words in Your presence will be, "Yes, Lord!" because I will then see the beautiful tapestry You were weaving with every person and event in my life, blessing me with Your plan. May we recognize Your divine appointments and be drawn to them, as You know the best plan for our lives. I pray my family and everyone who sees this tapestry will be reminded how Your hands work everything together for our good and for Your glory.

P

PATHS

Thank You for leading us along Your paths. May each time we see these paths be a reminder that You make our paths straight when we trust You with each detail in our lives and follow Your Word which says, *"Be careful to do what the Lord your God has commanded you; do not turn aside to the right or to the left"*

(Deut. 5:32). Thank You for Your promise to lead my family, friends, and me in the paths of righteousness.

We pray we will stay connected with You through prayer, attend a Bible-believing church, read Scripture, and live God-centered lives. We ask You for wisdom on our journey because You say You will direct us along paths of life and not destruction. Thank You, Lord, that You are the Author of life. As we walk these paths, I pray for every person to recognize Your voice and walk with You on Your path. May each person who walks Your path, O God, have their burden lifted and embrace the joy of Your presence.

If any of our family leaves Your path, Lord, convict their hearts and draw them back to You. Let the rest of the family discern their waywardness by Your Holy Spirit and gently through prayer work to guide the offender back to Your path and Your purpose for their life.

- *"You provide a broad path for my feet, so that my ankles do not give way"* (2 Sam. 22:37).

- *"Trust in the Lord with all your heart and lean not on your own understanding; in all your ways acknowledge him, and he will make your paths straight"* (Prov. 3:5-6).

- *"The path of the righteous is like the first gleam of dawn, shining ever brighter till the full light of day"* (Prov. 4:18).

- *"You have made known to me the path of life; you will fill me with joy in your presence, with eternal pleasures at your right hand"* (Ps. 16:11).

PETS

Gracious Lord, thank You for the pets You have given our family. Just as You have given humans dominion over the earth (Note: Gen. 1:26-27), You placed these pets in our care. Thank You for the joy and hours of happiness they bring us—and for the lessons they teach my children about responsibility, patience, and love. Lord, I pray we will genuinely care for these pets and that they will provide comfort and sweetness to our family. Let them always enjoy being in our home because You say, *"The godly care for their animals, but the wicked are always cruel"* (Prov. 12:10 NLT). Bless our pets with a sense of Your peace and presence, and help each one in our family to always care for our pets in a loving *manner.*

We ask that You will bless our cats, dogs or <u>*(name other pets)*</u> with good health and a long life. Thank You that You used an animal as an example of how we are to approach You in faith and ask for a miracle, just as a woman did for her daughter:

> *"He replied, 'It is not right to take the children's bread and toss it to their dogs.' 'Yes, Lord,' she said, 'but even the dogs eat the crumbs that fall from their masters' table.' Then Jesus answered, 'Woman, you have great faith! Your request is granted.' And her daughter was healed from that very hour"* (Matt. 15:26-28).

May we have the grace and faith to approach You in Your mighty power, even though the situation or request we have may seem monumental to us. Thank You that You are always approachable and willing to meet our every need eagerly and willingly (Note: Heb. 4:14-16).

PHONES

Lord, thank You for our phones. I ask Your blessing on each person who talks on this phone. I pray You will help each one to be very careful in what they say on this phone because You remind us not to use foul or abusive language. Let everything you say be good and helpful, so that your words will be an encouragement to those who hear them (Note: Eph. 4:29 NLT).

Lord, Your Word is full of reminders about the power of *speech*.

- *"When words are many, sin is not absent, but he who holds his tongue is wise"* (Prov. 10:19).

So I pray You will *"Set a guard over my mouth, O Lord; keep watch over the door of my lips"* (Ps. 141:3). We know our words are powerful, that we can speak life with *words*.

> *"From the fruit of his mouth a man's stomach is filled; with the harvest from his lips he is satisfied. The tongue has the power of life and death, and those who love it will eat its fruit"* (Prov. 18:20-21).

May You remind every person who uses this phone how powerful their words can be, to breathe life or death. May the communication over this phone be a life-giving source of blessing.

I ask that You will remind every person who uses this phone of Your truth, *"Those who control their tongue will have a long life; opening your mouth can ruin everything"* (Prov. 13:3 NLT). Help us guard our lips so we say only encouraging things to others. I ask what is in the heart of the one speaking will be a blessing to the person hearing because You say, *"out of the overflow of the heart, the mouth speaks"* (Matt. 12:34). Bless and anoint every person who talks on this phone to be used of You so what is spoken through it will honor You.

Father, You place great emphasis on our mouths and lips. You say *"'As for me, this is my covenant with them, says the Lord. 'My Spirit, who is on you, will not depart from you, and my words that I have put in your mouth will always be on your lips, on the lips of your children and on the lips of their descendants—from this time on and forever,' says the Lord"* (Isa. 59:21).

Teach us to value our mouths as You do. May the communication over this phone be a life-giving source of blessing.

- *"This observance will be for you like a sign on your hand and a reminder on your forehead that this law of the Lord is to be on your lips. For the Lord brought you out of Egypt with his mighty hand"* (Ex. 13:9).

- *"The word is very near you; it is in your mouth and in your heart so you may obey it"* (Deut. 30:14).

- *"Guard your tongue from profanity, and no more lying through your teeth"* (Ps. 34:13 MSG).

- *"Silence their lying lips—those proud and arrogant lips that accuse the godly"* (Ps. 31:18 NLT).

- *"You are fairer than the sons of men; grace is poured upon Your lips; therefore God has blessed You forever"* (Ps. 45:2 NASB).

- *"Open my lips, Lord, and my mouth will declare your praise"* (Ps. 51:15).

- *"With my lips I recount all the laws that come from your mouth"* (Ps. 119:13).

- *"Wisdom is found on the lips of the discerning, but a rod is for the back of one who has no sense"* (Prov. 10:13).

- *"The heart of the wise instructs his mouth and adds persuasiveness to his lips"* (Prov. 16:23 NASB).

"For it is good to keep these sayings in your heart and always ready on your lips" (Prov. 22:18 NLT).

PICTURES OF FRIENDS/NEIGHBORS

Thank You for this picture of friends. Thank You that this picture reminds me to pray for *(name the friends in the picture)*.

Cause our friendships to deepen over the years, and let each person in this picture be drawn to You and desire a relationship with You. If there is anyone in this picture who is not living a life that pleases You, keep them from being a bad influence on the others in this picture. Help them change their lives and seek You with all their heart so they won't be deceived. Give each person in this picture a good, wholesome, healthy character and good friendships. I pray You will connect with their hearts as their top priority and best friend.

Lord, I think of life-giving friendships mentioned in Your Word, like the friendship between David and Jonathan (Note: 1 Sam. 18) or between Jesus' disciples. You have even said that friends can be closer to us even than family (Note: Prov. 18:24). Thank You for providing me with like-minded friends who enrich my life and provide unique points of view that help me to grow spiritually. I pray You will continue to surround me with loyal friends who always direct me to You as my Comforter and not them.

When I talk with my friends, let our words and conversation be pleasing and glorifying to You. Cause us to refrain from idle gossip because *"Gracious words are a honeycomb, sweet to the soul and healing to the bones"* (Prov. 16:24) *"while a perverse person stirs up conflict, and a gossip separates close friends"* (Prov. 16:28).

PLANTS

Lord, as I pray Your blessing for these plants, I ask You to remind me of how alive Your Word is.

- *"For the word of God is alive and powerful. It is sharper than the sharpest two-edged sword, cutting between soul and spirit, between joint and marrow. It exposes our innermost thoughts and desires"* (Heb. 4:12 NLT).

If there are areas in my life or my family's lives that need pruning or improvement, use Your sharp Word to cut them away, just as we prune these plants so we may grow strong and *straight*.

Plants emit oxygen, which we need to breathe and live. Similarly, *"All Scripture is God-breathed and is useful for teaching, rebuking, correcting, and training in righteousness, so that the man of God may be thoroughly equipped for every good work"* (2 Tim. 3:16-17). May these plants remind us of Your Word that breathes life and truth into us. We ask You to fill every DNA cell, fiber, muscle, and ligament with Your breath, O God. May we grow as believers as we do every good work You want us to do (Note: Eph. 2:10).

- *"The land produced vegetation: plants bearing seed according to their kinds and trees bearing fruit with seed in it according to their kinds. And God saw that it was good"* (Gen. 1:12).

- *"Then our sons in their youth will be like well-nurtured plants, and our daughters will be like pillars carved to adorn a palace"* (Ps. 144:12).

PLATES/DISHES

Thank You, Lord, for our beautiful plates. As they hold our food, I pray You will sustain us with the best life has to offer as You have promised: *"I am the Lord your God ... Open wide your mouth and I will fill it"* (Ps. 81:10). As we handle these plates with our own hands, remind us that You said: *"See, I have engraved you on the palms of my hands"* (Isa. 49:16).

Give us the good sense to consume sensible portions of food from a balanced diet, so we might honor our bodies as temples of the Holy Spirit (Note: 1 Cor. 16:9). Strengthen our self-discipline in our eating, as Your Word says, *"Better a patient person than a warrior, one with self-control than one who takes a city"* (Prov. 16:32).

Thank You, Lord, for these plates made out of ceramic. Your Word reminds me that You are the Potter and I am the *clay*.

- *"O Lord, you are our Father. We are the clay, you are the potter; we are all the work of your hand"* (Isa. 64:8).

May every time we use these plates encourage us to be more conformed to Your image. May we be submitted to Your hand to mold us into a vessel that displays Your wonders.

- *"But we have this treasure in jars of clay to show that this all-surpassing power is from God and not from us"* (2 Cor. 4:7).

POSITIVE WORDS/MESSAGES

Lord, as we see pictures with a positive message we ask You to remind us to encourage one another. You tell us, *"Therefore*

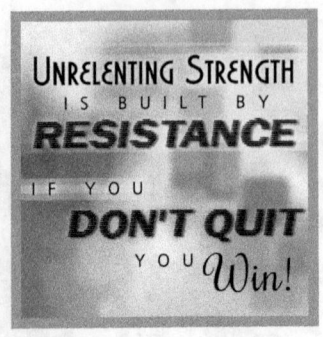

encourage one another and build each other up, just as in fact you are doing" (1 Thess. 5:11). May this picture remind us to encourage one another and build each other up as a physical or spiritual family. Help us to think and say only *"what is true, whatever is noble, whatever is right, whatever is pure, whatever is lovely, whatever is admirable—if anything is excellent or praiseworthy— think about such things"* (Phil. 4:8). We ask that our speech will be filled with thankfulness and gratefulness toward others (Note: Col. 4:6) and You. Please use these positive messages as a constant reminder to us that we are to offer others positive, encouraging, and life-giving *words*.

R

RIVERS/STREAMS

I speak out loud my thanks to You, Lord, for this river or stream and for Your promise.

> *"But those who drink the water I give will never be thirsty again. It becomes a fresh, bubbling spring within them, giving them eternal life"* (Jn. 4:14 NLT).

May everyone who sees this river or stream reflect on how You came to give life and give it to the fullest (Note: Jn. 10:10). I pray that You will remind my family and everyone who sees this river or stream that You are the only true satisfaction in life for them,  and they will never be thirsty again because of You. Give my family a thirst to learn more about You and Your character.

Thank You for the way this water reflects the future my family and I have with *You:*

- "Then the angel showed me a river with the water of life, clear as crystal, flowing from the throne of God and of the Lamb" (Rev. 22:1 NLT).

- "They are like trees planted along the riverbank, bearing fruit each season. Their leaves never wither, and they prosper in all they do" (Ps. 1:3 NLT).

- "They feast on the abundance of your house; you give them drink from your river of delights" (Ps. 36:8).

- "A river brings joy to the city of our God, the sacred home of the Most High" (Ps. 46:4 NLT).

- "Anyone who is thirsty may come to me! Anyone who believes in me may come and drink! For the Scriptures declare, 'Rivers of living water will flow from his heart'" (Jn. 7:37-39 NLT).

ROADS

May we always walk on the road You want for our lives so we are not hurt by difficult, hard roads. Lord, I pray especially for the younger people in my family, my extended family, and friends. Show them firm, level paths for their feet, and may they always walk in Your ways (Prov. 4:26). Thank You for reminding us in Your Scripture *"for a man's ways are in full view of the Lord, and he examines all his paths"* (Prov. 5:21). Examine the road we are on, Lord, and show us how to correct wrong turns or dangers ahead through Your Word, Your Holy Spirit within us, other people, and through answers to prayer.

Bless every person who sees this road. Remind them to walk on Your road, because You say, *"The path of the righteous is like the first gleam of dawn, shining ever brighter till the full light of day. But the way of the wicked is like deep darkness; they do not know what makes them stumble"* (Prov. 4:18-19). Use this road to remind everyone who sees it of Your truth, Lord, and the need to live consistently with the principles and morals in the Bible.

- *"So be very careful to act exactly as God commands you. Don't veer off to the right or the left. Walk straight down the road God commands so that you'll have a good life and live a long time in the land that you're about to possess"* (Deut. 5:32 MSG).

- *"You have made known to me the path of life; you will fill me with joy in your presence, with eternal pleasures at your right hand"* (Ps. 16:11).

- *"You broaden the path beneath me, so that my ankles do not turn"* (Ps. 18:36).

ROCKS

Gracious heavenly Father, as I look at this rock, I thank You that it depicts strength and solidness. It reminds me that You alone are my strength and an unmovable Rock on whom I can depend. Thank You for being my family's solid Rock and the Rock in whom I can trust.

O Lord, as I think of how stable and solid rocks are, it reminds me of how unstable and shifting my family's lives can be—especially our children as they grow and develop. I pray that each one of us, especially *(name one or more of your children),* will find their total identity in You and not in anything this world has to offer or in anyone else who claims to have the answers.

Help them to understand their security, worth, and purpose as a person is found in following You. You provide a stable, unfailing love. Help us not to value our worth as a person based upon the shifting opinions of people. May *(child's name)* understand the unique qualities You have placed inside them and see themselves as You do—a beautiful, special person. Each time we see this rock, let it remind us of You and Your unchanging love, You are our rock (Note: Ps. 18:2).

As we live our daily lives, help us to use the truth of Your *Word:*

- *"He lifted me out of the slimy pit, out of the mud and mire; he set my feet on a rock and gave me a firm place to stand"* (Ps. 40:2).

- *"May the words of my mouth and the meditation of my heart be pleasing in your sight, O Lord, my Rock and my Redeemer"* (Ps. 19:14).

- *"He is the Rock, his works are perfect, and all his ways are just. A faithful God who does no wrong, upright and just is he"* (Deut. 32:4).

- *"Then he told his family members, 'Gather some stones.' So they gathered stones and piled them in a heap. Then

Jacob and Laban sat down beside the pile of stones to eat a covenant meal" (Gen. 31:46 NLT).

- "But his bow remained steady, his strong arms stayed limber, because of the hand of the Mighty One of Jacob, because of the Shepherd, the Rock of Israel" (Gen. 49:24).

- "There is no one holy like the Lord; there is no one besides you; there is no Rock like our God" (1 Sam. 2:2).

- "The Lord is my rock and my fortress and my deliverer, My God, my rock, in whom I take refuge; My shield and the horn of my salvation, my stronghold" (Ps. 18:2 NASB).

- "And the rain fell, and the floods came, and the winds blew and slammed against that house; and yet it did not fall, for it had been founded on the rock" (Matt. 7:25 NASB).

S

SEA/SEASHORE

Great Creator, as we look at the sea, we are reminded that You made everything in the heavens, the earth, and all things in the sea (Note: Prov. 8:1-29). "*God called the dry ground land and the waters seas. And God saw that it was good*" (Gen. 1:10). Thank You for being our protection, even in the most dangerous of situations.

❧ *"God is our refuge and strength, always ready to help in times of trouble. So we will not fear when earthquakes come and the mountains crumble into the sea"* (Ps. 46:1,2 NLT).

Remind every person who looks at this picture of the sea or  seashore that the Creator of the universe is also keenly interested in them and loves them. Thank You for the safety we have in You—that we are always in Your care.

❧ *"You faithfully answer our prayers with awesome deeds, O God our savior. You are the hope of everyone on earth, even those who sail on distant seas"* (Ps. 65:5 NLT).

El Shaddai ("SHAD-I," strong one), thank You that You reign over all Your creation.

❧ *"He will rule from sea to sea and from the River to the ends of the earth"* (Ps. 72:8).

Your power amazes me, El Shaddai. As I see the sand by the ocean, it reminds me of how You are always thinking about me.

❧ *"How precious to me are your thoughts, O God! How vast is the sum of them! Were I to count them, they would outnumber the grains of sand. When I awake, I am still with you"* (Ps. 139:17-18).

Thank You, Lord, that You direct all of nature according to Your *plan:*

- *"He set the earth on its foundations; it can never be moved. You covered it with the deep as with a garment; the waters stood above the mountains. But at your rebuke the waters fled, at the sound of your thunder they took to flight; they flowed over the mountains, they went down into the valleys, to the place you assigned for them. You set a boundary they cannot cross; never again will they cover the earth"* (Ps. 104:5-9).

Thank You that I am always in Your thoughts and that You are always with *me.*

SHEEP/LAMBS

Lord Jesus, thank You that You are *"the Lamb of God who takes away the sin of the world."* (Jn. 1:29 NLT). Remind us that You are the Lamb who was slain for the creation of the world (Note: Rev. 13:8). Jesus, You are the worthy Lamb. *"In a loud voice they were saying: 'Worthy is the Lamb, who was slain, to receive power and wealth and wisdom and strength and honor and glory and praise'"* (Rev. 5:12).

Lord, as I see these sheep now, it reminds me that I am one of Your sheep. Thank You that we are cared for, protected, and loved by You as our gentle Shepherd. You provide our every need: physical, spiritual, emotional, intellectual, and financial (Note: Ps. 23). Help us to listen closely to Your voice and follow Your lead. If we wander away from You, Jehovah Raah ("the Lord is my Shepherd"), lead us back quickly, speaking to us through Your Word, through Christian friends, godly counsel, circumstances, or painful situations. Let us be thankful and realize every good gift comes from You (Note: Jas. 1:17).

I pray for _(name someone in your family, extended family or of your friends who either is wandering away or has a tendency toward wandering away)._ Thank You that by faith we believe You will bring _(name this person)_ back into a close relationship with You as the Good Shepherd because You say, "I am the good shepherd; I know my sheep and they know me" (Jn. 10:14). May You do what is necessary for this person to have a restored relationship with You as the Good Shepherd.

- *"The gatekeeper opens the gate for him, and the sheep recognize his voice and come to him. He calls his own sheep by name and leads them out. After he has gathered his own flock, he walks ahead of them, and they follow him because they know his voice"* (Jn. 10:3-4 NLT).

- *"For this is what the Sovereign Lord says: I myself will search and find my sheep. I will be like a shepherd looking for his scattered flock. I will find my sheep and rescue them from all the places where they were scattered on that dark and cloudy day. I myself will tend my sheep and give them a place to lie down in peace, says the Sovereign Lord. I will search for my lost ones who strayed away, and I will bring them safely home again. I will bandage the injured and strengthen the weak. But I will destroy those who are fat and powerful. I will feed them, yes— feed them justice!"* (Ezek. 34:11-12, 15-16 NLT).

- *"I am the good shepherd; I know my sheep and my sheep know me"* (Jn. 10:14).

SHOES

Lord, as I look at these shoes, I pray that every step we take will be consistent with Your will for our lives. Help my family, friends, and me to stay on the straight path You have individually designed for us, *"for small is the gate and narrow the road that leads to life, and only a few find it"* (Matt. 7:14). You tell us … *"and walk in love, just as Christ also loved you and gave Himself* up for us, an offering and a sacrifice to God as a fragrant aroma" (Eph. 5:2 NASB). I pray that my family's every step in these shoes will be with love in their hearts that comes out through their lips (Note: Matt. 12:33) and be exactly what You would do, Lord, if You were walking in these shoes. Please make my path straight and protect me by making me as surefooted as a deer, enabling me to stand on mountain heights (Note: Ps. 18:33 NLT).

May we each walk in Your ways as a habitual lifestyle, and help us to walk humbly with You in these shoes.

> "He has showed you, O man, what is good. And what does the Lord require of you? To act justly and to love mercy and to walk humbly with your God" (Mic. 6:8).

May we stand firm in the shoes of the Gospel of peace (Note: Eph. 6:15), which allow us to walk with You every day.

> "For you have rescued me from death; you have kept my feet from slipping. So now I can walk in your presence, O God, in your life-giving light" (Ps. 56:13 NLT).

> "How beautiful on the mountains are the feet of the messenger who brings good news, the good news of peace and salvation, the news that the God of Israel reigns!" (Isa. 52:7 NLT).

SKY

Thank You, Lord, for creating the heavens and the earth (Note: Gen. 1). I am awed when I think of how big the universe really is, how diverse it is, and how creative You are to make it all from nothing. Yet You are closely involved with every aspect of my family, friends, and life—no detail is too small. You love to notice and care about it all.

> *"When I look at the night sky and see the work of your fingers—the moon and the stars you set in place—what are mere mortals that you should think about them, human beings that you should care for them?"* (Ps. 8:3-4 NLT).

When we see the sky, remind us that You are in control of everything and You care for us. Help us to pray and praise You more, O God, Creator of the universe.

The sky is a constant reminder of protection—the atmosphere of our planet is the very thing that keeps us alive and that allows life to flourish here. May it remind us of the protection we have when we follow You, even though we often don't consider it or even think about it.

The sky can be a place of serene calm through clouds, a place of refreshment through rain, or even a place of terror through severe weather like hurricanes and tornadoes. Let these characteristics remind us of the many facets of Your personality—like grace, mercy, and love—but let us never lose sight of the atmosphere You created.

SOFA

Heavenly Father, thank You for rest. It is such an essential part of our experience on this earth, and we are grateful for every chance we have to sit down and rest, whether it be for a few moments or for an extended period of time. This sofa is a

place where we can rest—relax with a book, watch some media, play a game, or have deep conversations with family or friends. As we do so, we pray You will bless the time we spend on this sofa. We anoint it for Your purposes.

As we entertain company on this sofa, remind us of Your Word, which says, *"Keep on loving each other as brothers. Do not forget* to entertain strangers, for by so doing some people have entertained angels without knowing it" (Heb. 13:1-2).

When we recline on this sofa for a moment of relaxation, let us take to heart Your Word, which says, *"Relax, everything's going to be all right; rest, everything's coming together; open your hearts, love is on the way"* (Jude 1 MSG).

SPORTS EQUIPMENT/ MEMORABILIA/TROPHIES

SPORTS EQUIPMENT

Thank You, Lord, for the sports equipment we have and for the hours of fun we enjoy together playing sports. I ask Your blessing and safety on the people who use this equipment. I pray that my family, my extended family, and our friends will be reminded of the truth that, *"All athletes are disciplined in their training. They do it to win a prize that will fade away, but we do it for an eternal prize. So I run with purpose in every step"* (1 Cor. 9:25,26 NLT).

Thank You that with Your help, O God, we can run with purpose in every step (Note: Heb. 12:1). Show us the specific race You have for each one of our lives.

We ask Your anointing and blessing on everyone who will use this equipment, and we anoint this sports equipment to be used by You in our lives.

Thank You for the ability to be involved in sports, to see sports, and to enjoy sports. We ask for protection, relaxation, and strength of character to develop through the various sports or activities in which we are involved. Teach us self-discipline in all areas of our lives.

Sports Memorabilia/Trophies

Thank You also, Lord, for the sports memorabilia my family and I have in this home. I thank You for the positive experiences received through earning trophies. But even so, remind me that trophies, ribbons, autographs, or _(fill in the blank with a sports memorabilia item)_ will one day fade into the background compared with the wonderful rewards my family and I will have in Your presence. As we see this memorabilia, may it cause my family, my extended family, and me to reflect on Your rewards.

> *"You are worthy, our Lord and God, to receive glory and honor and power, for you created all things, and by your will they were created and have their being"* (Rev. 4:11).

Lord, as I see the trophies and medals my children have earned, it reminds me to thank You for their God-given gifts, talents, and physical health. Thank You for the awards they have received, I pray that every time they see this reward for hard work, it will remind them to be just as disciplined in seeking Your reward as they were in earning these trophies and medals.

You say, *"And without faith it is impossible to please God, because anyone who comes to him must believe that he exists and that he rewards those who earnestly seek him"* (Heb. 11:6). So I pray Your blessing and anointing on these trophies and medals to remind my child to seek You and Your reward as the top priority throughout their lives.

STARS

Father, the stars in the sky are just one more reminder of how awesome and great Your creative abilities are. I love to look at them just to think about how great You are. Lord, let us not forget to honor You as Creator of all that exists.

- *"It is I who made the earth and created mankind on it. My own hands stretched out the heavens; I marshaled their starry hosts"* (Isa. 45:12).

We know that the stars are used for navigation, fixed in the heavens as guiding lights on earth. As we look at these stars, let them be a reminder to search out Your will and purposes for us in Your Word, which will also guide and help us navigate if we take the time to seek. We are in awe of Your majesty and grandeur; we are in awe that You are so loving and care so deeply about us.

- *"When I consider your heavens, the works of your fingers, the moon and the stars, which you have set in place"* (Ps. 8:3).

- *"The Lord merely spoke, and the heavens were created. He breathed the word, and all the stars were born"* (Ps. 33:6 NLT).

- *"The moon and stars to rule by night, for his loving kindness is everlasting"* (Ps. 139:6 NASB).

From my earthly perspective, the stars in the sky are limitless. But from Your view:

- *"He determines the number of the stars and calls them each by name"* (Ps. 147:4).

- *"He is the Maker of the Bear and Orion, the Pleiades and the constellations of the south. He performs wonders that cannot be fathomed, miracles that cannot be counted"* (Job 9:9-10).

- *"And also carefully guard yourselves so that you don't look up into the skies and see the sun and moon and stars, all the constellations of the skies, and be seduced into worshiping and serving them. God set them out for everybody's benefit, everywhere. But you—God took you right out of the iron furnace, out of Egypt, to become the people of his inheritance— and that's what you are this very day"* (Deut. 4:15 MSG).

STAIRS/STEPS

We know our journey through life will be filled with many stairs that are crooked, steep, and sometimes treacherous. Other times the climb will be easy. Help us to remember to praise You whether it is difficult or easy.

- *"Consider it all joy, my brethren, when you encounter various trials, knowing that the testing of your faith produces endurance"* (Jas. 1:2-3 NASB).

Let us remember that our goal is to climb closer to You in all of our activities, thoughts, and actions. Remind us to read Your Word more often, because Your Word draws us closer to You.

- *"Whoever has my commands and obeys them, he is the one who loves me. He who loves me will be loved by my Father, and I too will love him and show myself to him"* (Jn. 14:21).

You are with us daily as we climb the steps of life; make us as surefooted as a deer (Note: 2 Sam. 22:34; Ps. 18:33). We pray that as we climb these steps, You will protect us when we fall and make mistakes as we go through life.

Lord, as my children or friends climb these stairs, let them be reminded how blessed they are to be able to walk up and down stairs and to enjoy good health. We ask that You continue to bless us with good health and allow us to continue to share information about how gracious You are, O God. We pray You will continue to give us strength to climb the stairs, not just in this house but the stairs of life.

Heavenly Father, may we always keep our sights set on You, striving and reaching for higher goals to elevate our lives in such manner that we honor You. As we climb the stairs of life, strengthen us, help us persevere, and *"Let us not become weary in doing good, for at the proper time we will reap a harvest if we do not give up"* (Gal. 6:9).

- *"The steps of a good man are ordered by the Lord, and He delights in his way"* (Ps. 37:23 NKJV).

- *"The Sovereign Lord is my strength! He makes me as surefooted as a deer, able to tread upon the heights"* (Hab. 3:19 NLT).

- *"Direct my footsteps according to your word; let no sin rule over me"* (Ps. 119:133).

- *"In their hearts humans plan their course, but the Lord establishes their steps"* (Prov. 16:9).

STATUES

As I look at statues, they remind me of Your Word, where You say, *"You shall not make for yourself an idol in the form of anything in heaven above or on the earth beneath or in the waters below"* (Ex. 20:4). I pray that nothing will take the place of You in my family, my friends, or in my heart. While we are not consciously tempted to bow down to statues or idols, protect us from idolatry in our hearts because Your Word says, *"Put to death, therefore, whatever belongs to your earthly nature: sexual immorality, impurity, lust, evil desires and greed, which is idolatry"* (Col. 3:5). Bring to my attention anything that has become an idol in my life, and preserve me from dedicating more of my resources to such things.

May we find Your power in giving us the victory over spiritual idolatry in its many forms every day—giving our focused attention and allegiance to anything or anyone but You alone because You say, *"Dear children, keep away from anything that might take God's place in your hearts"* (1 Jn. 5:21 NLT).

STEREO/CD PLAYER/ IPOD™/AUDIO DEVICES

Heavenly Father, music is a wonderful gift from You, and we thank You as it brings us hours of joy. I pray as music is  played over this stereo, computer, iPod™, or radio, it will bring uplifting encouragement to my family, friends, and me. As I pray for Your blessing on this stereo, computer, iPod™, or radio now, it reminds me how You have used music in the lives of others.

> *"And whenever the tormenting spirit from God troubled Saul, David would play the harp. Then Saul would feel better, and the tormenting spirit would go away"* (1 Sam. 16:23 NLT).

I pray we will feel encouraged and uplifted because of the music we hear through this stereo. If any of the music we hear contains offensive, profane, or blasphemous lyrics, I pray You will bring it to our attention so we can remove it from our home. I ask You remove it from our hearts. May Your blessing be on the music we play in our home.

> *"Is any one of you in trouble? He should pray. Is anyone happy? Let him sing songs of praise"* (Jas. 5:13).

- *"Sing to the Lord a new song, his praise from the ends of the earth, you who go down to the sea, and all that is in it, you islands, and all who live in them. Let the desert and its towns raise their voices; let the settlements where Kedar lives rejoice. Let the people of Sela sing for joy; let them shout from the mountaintops"* (Isa. 42:10-11).

- *"The Lord your God is with you, he is mighty to save. He will take great delight in you, he will quiet you with his love, he will rejoice over you with singing"* (Zeph. 3:17).

- *"After consulting the people, Jehoshaphat appointed men to sing to the Lord and to praise him for the splendor of his holiness as they went out at the head of the army, saying: 'Give thanks to the Lord, for his love endures forever.' As they began to sing and praise, the Lord set ambushes against the men of Ammon and Moab and Mount Seir who were invading Judah, and they were defeated"* (2 Chron. 20:21-22).

Whenever struggles come, remind us of who You are and help us to begin singing praises to You even before we see the victory—just as Jehoshaphat did! Thank You for the gift of music; use it in our lives to demonstrate and fuel our faith in You (Note: Eph. 5:19). Thank You, heavenly Father, for singing over my family, extended family, friends, and me with Your wonderful love. Every time we hear music, may we be reminded of how much You delight in us and rejoice over us with *singing*.

- *"Sing for joy in the Lord, O you righteous ones; Praise is becoming to the upright. Give thanks to the Lord with the lyre; Sing praises to Him with a harp of ten strings. Sing to Him a new song; Play skillfully with a shout of joy"* (Ps. 33:1-3 NASB).

- *"Then I will sing praises to your name forever as I fulfill my vows each day"* (Ps. 61:8 NLT).

- *"My Strength, I sing praise to you; you, O God, are my fortress, my loving God"* (Ps. 59:17).

- *"I wash my hands to declare my innocence. I come to your altar, O Lord, singing a song of thanksgiving and telling of all your wonders"* (Ps. 26:6-7 NLT).

- *"My heart is breaking as I remember how it used to be: I walked among the crowds of worshipers, leading a great procession to the house of God, singing for joy and giving thanks amid the sound of a great celebration! But each day the Lord pours his unfailing love upon me, and through each night I sing his songs, praying to God who gives me life"* (Ps. 42:4, 8 NLT).

- *"The Lord is my strength and my shield; my heart trusts in him, and I am helped. My heart leaps for joy and I will give thanks to him in song"* (Ps. 28:7).

SUN

Thank You, Lord, that Your Word says, *"From the rising of the sun to the place where it sets, the name of the Lord is to be praised"*

(Ps. 113:3). I praise You now for another day of life, of seeing the sun, and of feeling its heat (Note: Ps. 19:6). Thank You for placing the sun in the sky, and for Your creative genius. *"May His name endure forever; may it continue as long as the sun"* (Ps. 72:17). As the sun always shines, regardless of whether we see it or not, let us remember that You are always present in our lives, whether we feel Your presence or not.

Thank You for Your great love that is new every *morning*.

- *"Because of the Lord's great love we are not consumed, for his compassions never fail. They are new every morning; great is your faithfulness"* (Lam. 3:22-23).
- *"My heart joins in saying, Praise him, sun and moon, praise him, all you shining stars"* (Ps. 148:3).

T

TABLE

Jehovah Shammah (the Lord is present), thank You that You are always present at the table with us. You are right here with us and that You will always be with us because God has said, *"Never will I leave you, never will I forsake you"* (Heb. 13:5).

So because You are always with us, *"we will fear no evil. You prepare a table before us and cause our cups to overflow"* (Ps. 23:5).

We invite You now to our table, Lord, because Your Word says, *"Here I am! I stand at the door and knock. If anyone hears my voice and opens the door, I will come in and eat with him, and he with me"* (Rev. 3:20). May each person who eats at this table recognize You are here at our table.

Thank You for the fellowship that happens around this table, the delightful work of building relationships with our family  and friends we invite to share a meal with us. We pray every word spoken in conversation around this table will glorify You. We ask You will unite our hearts as we dine, talk, and laugh. Blessed be Your name, Lord.

> *"For who is greater, the one who is at the table or the one who serves? Is it not the one who is at the table? But I am among you as one who serves. You are those who have stood by me in my trials. And I confer on you a kingdom, just as my Father conferred one on me, so that you may eat and drink at my table in my kingdom and sit on thrones, judging the twelve tribes of Israel"* (Lk. 22:27-30).

> *"Is not the cup of thanksgiving for which we give thanks a participation in the blood of Christ? And is not the bread that we break a participation in the body of Christ?"* (1 Cor. 10:16)

TELEVISION/DVD PLAYER

Lord, as I look at this television now, I am reminded of how much time my family spends watching various programs. I pray Your protection for my children and me.

> *"I will be careful to live a blameless life—when will you come to help me? I will lead a life of integrity in my own home. I will refuse to look at anything vile and vulgar"* (Ps. 101:2-3 NLT).

I pray that nothing inappropriate or unwholesome will be viewed through this television. *"Turn my eyes away from worthless things; preserve my life according to Your word"* (Ps. 119:37).

Lord, I pray that we will use our television and DVD player for good viewing, for educational purposes—not watching gossip shows or living vicariously through reality shows, sitcoms, or soap operas. I pray we will be drawn to positive, uplifting programs and movies, single-minded in our desires to be pure as a family. Thank You that we can use our television and DVD player for good purposes that please You and help us in our lives. I pray whatever we view on this television will be something that will help us cling to our faith in Christ, and keep our conscience clear (Note: 1 Tim. 1:19). May Your blessing be on all who watch our television and DVD player.

- *"Whatever is true, whatever is noble, whatever is right, whatever is pure, whatever is lovely, whatever is admirable—if anything is excellent or praiseworthy—think about such things"* (Phil. 4:8).

- *"Therefore, with minds that are alert and fully sober, set your hope on the grace to be brought to you when Jesus Christ is revealed at his coming. As obedient children, do not conform to the evil desires you had when you lived in ignorance. But just as he who called you is holy, so be holy in all you do; for it is written: 'Be holy, because I am holy'"* (1 Pet. 1:13-16).

TOYS

Thank You, Lord, for our child's toys. Thank You for the special memories we have in our family because of these toys. Bless

and encourage my child as they grow into the person You want them to be.

For our younger children, I pray they will play with their toys nicely and develop traits like sharing, self-discipline, connecting with other children, and giving to others of what You have given to them. May my children have courteous, gracious hearts that generously give and share with others. May You provide me with teachable moments as I play with my child, and use me to bless, help, encourage and train my child in the exceedingly great value of knowing You and living according to Your Word.

- *"Jesus said, 'Let the little children come to me, and do not hinder them, for the kingdom of heaven belongs to such as these'"* (Matt. 19:14).

- *"Delight yourself in the Lord and he will give you the desires of your heart"* (Ps. 37:4).

- *"I tell you the truth, unless you change and become like little children, you will never enter the kingdom of heaven. Therefore, whoever humbles himself like this child is the greatest in the kingdom of heaven"* (Matt. 18:3-4).

- *"Train a child in the way he should go, and when he is old he will not turn from it"* (Prov. 22:6).

- *"Fix these words of mine in your hearts and minds; tie them as symbols on your hands and bind them on your foreheads. Teach them to your children, talking about them when you sit at home and when you walk along the road, when you lied down and when you get up"* (Deut. 11:18-19)

- *"Teach me to do your will, for you are my God; may your good Spirit lead me on level ground"* (Ps. 143:10).

V

VESSELS/VASES

Lord, as I see these vases, I pray You will use me as Your vessel, as Your precious child, and fill my heart and life with Your love, Scriptures, and light. You tell my family and me that You want us to:

> *"... have the power to understand, as all God's people should, how wide, how long, how high, and how deep his love is. May you experience the love of Christ, though it is too great to understand fully. Then you will be made complete with all the fullness of life and power that comes from God"* (Eph. 3:18-19 NLT).

Lord, as this vase is filled with life in the form of plants and flowers, may You fill my family with Your abundant life (Note: Jn. 10:10). Just as the plants and flowers in this vase are nourished with water, I pray You will nourish my family with Your living water, which is Your grace that cleanses us, provides us with spiritual life, and gives us Your transforming Holy Spirit (Note: Jn. 7:38-39). As the

plants and flowers in this vase require sunshine to grow, we pray we will bask in the sunshine of Your love, allowing Your vastness and completeness to warm our hearts and lives (Note: Jn. 4; Eph. 3:18-19). As we watch various plants grow in these vases, remind us that every living thing grows, and that You want us to *"grow in the grace and knowledge of our Lord and Savior Jesus Christ"* (2 Pet. 3:18).

Vessels are ideal containers, useful tools for transporting things from one place to another. Thank You that You use each member of our family as Your vessel. Please use me as Your vessel because You say, *"But we have this treasure in earthen vessels, so that the surpassing greatness of the power will be of God and not from ourselves"* (2 Cor. 4:7 NASB). Mold us with Your Words in the Bible to be Your vessels, *Lord*.

WATER

Lord, water is an essential part of life. We are washed with water when we are born and washed again when we die. When we are baptized, we are immersed in water as a covenant experience of being buried with Christ and coming back to life.

We continually need to drink water for our bodies to replenish cells in all our organs. Thank You for the water in this home to shower, wash our hands, and to drink. Thank You for water because it makes our planet inhabitable. Most of all, thank You that You are Living Water.

I'm reminded of Your encounter with the Samaritan woman at the well (Note: Jn. 4:1-42). You told her, *"If you knew the gift of God, and who it is who says to you, 'Give Me a drink,' you would have asked Him, and He would have given you living water"* (Jn. 4:10 NASB). Lord, I ask that You would remind us of Your presence as our Living Water each time we use the shower or sink. Thank You that the well of Living Water will never run dry.

Lord, as I look at water, it causes me to reflect on Your *promise*.

- *"Jesus replied, 'Anyone who drinks this water will soon become thirsty again. But those who drink the water I give will never be thirsty again. It becomes a fresh, bubbling spring within them, giving them eternal life'"* (Jn. 4:14 NLT).

I pray that You will remind my family and everyone who uses water in this home that You are the only true satisfaction in life.

Jesus, You walked on the water that You created (Note: Matt. 14:22-31). You commanded the waves to cease, and they did (Note: Matt. 8:23-27). You are greater than the deepest ocean. You are stronger than the swiftest rapids. You are more powerful than the largest waves.

Water is so refreshing and life giving to us. It reminds me of what You said about Yourself: Anyone who is thirsty may come to me! Anyone who believes in me may come and drink! For the Scriptures declare, *"Rivers of living water will flow from his heart"* (Jn. 7:37-39 NLT). When He said "living water" in this verse, Jesus was speaking of the Spirit, who would be given to everyone believing in Him.

Thank You for giving the Holy Spirit to us because of our relationship with You. Thank You for the refreshing life You give.

I pray now for every member of my family to know the joy of hearing from the Holy Spirit and being with You *forever.*

- *"They will never again be hungry or thirsty; they will never be scorched by the heat of the sun"* (Rev. 7:16 NLT).
- *"The words of a man's mouth are deep waters, but the fountain of wisdom is a bubbling brook"* (Prov. 18:4).

- *"And if you give even a cup of cold water to one of the least of my followers, you will surely be rewarded"* (Matt. 10:42 NLT).

- *"When they came up out of the water, the Spirit of the Lord snatched Philip away; and the eunuch no longer saw him, but went on his way rejoicing"* (Acts 8:39 NASB).

- *"The Spirit and the bride say, 'Come!' And let him who hears say, 'Come!' Whoever is thirsty, let him come; and whoever wishes, let him take the free gift of the water of life"* (Rev. 22:17).

WINDOWS

Lord, windows provide protection from the elements—rain, wind, heat, and cold. They also allow much-needed sunlight and refreshing breezes to enter our homes and blow away stagnant air that has become stale and depleted. I pray over these windows now, both as an entrance of light and air into my home. I call them anointed and declare that no evil thing shall pass through them. Just as they provide access to welcome breezes and healing, warming sunlight, let us open the windows of our souls to the wind of Your Holy Spirit and the light of Your Word.

- *"Some men came, bringing to [Jesus] a paralyzed man, carried by four of them. Since they could not get him to Jesus because of the crowd, they made an opening in the roof above Jesus by digging through it and then lowered the mat the man was lying on. When Jesus saw their faith, he said to the paralyzed man, 'Son, your sins are forgiven'"* (Mark 2:3-5).

- *"He sends his word and melts them; he stirs up his breezes, and the waters flow"* (Ps. 147:18).

- *"Suddenly a sound like the blowing of a violent wind came from heaven and filled the whole house where they were sitting. They saw what seemed to be tongues of fire that separated and came to rest on each of them. All of them were filled with the Holy Spirit and began to speak in other tongues as the Spirit enabled them"* (Acts 2:2-4).

WORK DESKS

Lord, thank You for this desk and all the work that is accomplished on it. I pray Your blessing on the work that is done at this desk and the calls that are made. I ask that they will be conducted in a manner pleasing to You. We pray especially that we will remember You as we work,

- *"Whatever you do, work at it with all your heart, as working for the Lord, not for men"* (Col. 3:23).

Lord, help me to give my best effort at my work, whether in an office environment or working in the home.

> "*But as for you, be strong and courageous, for your work will be rewarded*" (2 Chron. 15:7 NLT).

Thank You, Lord, that work was created by You. Thank You that meaningful work is Your idea, and You say that work is good.

> "*The Lord God took the man and put him in the Garden of Eden to work it and take care of it*" (Gen. 2:15).

Whatever work is done at this desk, bless the person working to focus with concentrated effort to accomplish the task. Your Scriptures say, "*All hard work brings a profit, but mere talk leads only to poverty*" (Prov. 14:23).

I ask that the work will be enjoyable, and the work will be used by You to bless and encourage others—even if the person working views it as hard and unfulfilling. Turn the heart of the workman to the purpose of the task as unto the Lord.

> *"And whatever you do, do it heartily, as to the Lord and not to men, knowing that from the Lord you will receive the reward of the inheritance; for you serve the Lord Christ"* (Col 3:23-24 NKJV).

I pray Your blessing and grace to be on every person who works at this desk, Lord.

MEET THE AUTHOR

NATALIE S. WOLFE has dedicated years to learning about how the Lord loves to bless and heal His people. She completed the intensive Christian Healing Certification Program by Randy Clark through Global Awakening. This curriculum was focused on inner healing as well as physical healing. In 2016, Natalie completed the Healing School and was ordained through Joan Hunter Ministries.

The founder and president of Wolfe Real Estate Company, Natalie's background in real estate provides her with unique knowledge and experience on how to pray over and bless your home. She has facilitated numerous Bible studies and does speaking and counseling for groups on how to bless your home to invite God's blessing.

Natalie worked in commercial real estate for 27 years as a top producer where she leased, sold, and developed office buildings in Kansas City and throughout the Midwest with the largest commercial real estate company in the world.

Natalie was one of the first women in commercial real estate in Kansas City and broke many records for production with a reputation for integrity. She was the first woman to join the elite national organization for real estate, SIOR in Kansas City.

Known for her financial acumen, her creative approach to real estate problems, and for creating opportunities for investors to gain "land territory," Natalie was trusted by many national Fortune 500 corporations.

Natalie is the founder of Your Family Blessings, LLC, and is committed to training others how to put a shield around their homes and families and invite God's favor and protection to regain their territory and receive their God-ordained blessings.

If you would like to learn more or to invite Natalie Wolfe to speak for your group or organization, please visit:

www.ABCBLESSING.com

www.ingramcontent.com/pod-product-compliance
Lightning Source LLC
LaVergne TN
LVHW051543070426
835507LV00021B/2377